THE LAW ILLUSION

ANALYTIC ESSAYS
FOR THE WORKING PUBLIC
ON THE FRAUD CALLED
"COMMON LAW" DECISIONS

Compiled by Valeriano Diviacchi

ISBN:

9780692582923

Library of Congress
Control Number:
2016907750

Printed in the United
States of America

Second Printing

For information or to order additional books,
Please write:

Diviacchi Promotions, Inc.
Boston, MA.
617-542-3175

Or visit our website and online catalogue at www.diviacchi.com

About the essay authors:

The names of the attorney authors were removed, changed, or pseudonyms used in order to avoid retribution from the supposed protectors of free speech who call themselves judges before whom they practice.

I dedicate this book to all solo trial attorneys practicing with honesty, forthrightness, and a sense of justice and who therefore are desperately trying to survive in the American system of injustice. In a courtroom full of liars, the honest man is not king but a threat.

TABLE OF CONTENTS

BOOK I / OTHER ESSAYS

There is no such thing as justice - in or out of court.

Clarence Darrow

I.   PROLOGUE

For Americans, regardless of one's religion if any, fear of the law has replaced fear of God or the gods as the ultimate arbitrator of right and wrong in life. This transformation of the law into a secular god is a substantive change in the nature of Western Civilization, especially for the working class and most of the middle class. The law has never been and never will be a friend of the working class nor of most of the middle class. It either supports or stands by idly while wage slavery takes over the world economy in the same way that it supported or ignored chattel slavery for millenia.

Instead of serving as a pragmatic tool for efficient commerce and for avoidance of the social harm caused by private feuding, the law has become a secular god creating feuds to replace those solved by technology in order to assure adequate worshipers for its outdated and oligarchical techniques. It is a contradiction in theory and in practice: a secular religious normative system for enforcing hidden ethics and morals that have nothing to do with commerce or private feuds. As argued by many philosophers and theologians such as T.S. Eliot who are behind the scope of this essay, a society lacking the wisdom of a successful religious tradition emphasizing spiritual concerns to counterbalance the worldly ambitions of secular government will degenerate into tyranny, social and cultural dysfunction, and fragmentation. Unknowing or knowingly, to avoid this, the powers of the law are transforming law into a secular religion. However, can secular religion be a counterbalance to secular tyranny, dysfunction, and fragmentation?

In prior periods of social change, workers always had at least one alternative other than the law for social and moral support: usually a religion or family. Religious support has been negated by the law as a secular religion. Family support is fairly quickly becoming meaningless now that the majority of Americans have never been married and given that, for those workers who have children and try to support them, of these children 40% will be born to unwed mothers, 22% will live in poverty for their entire childhood (40% will have at least one year of poverty), and 25% will never have a father in the family. It is only a matter of time before the majority of workers live alone and children are either a luxury for the few that can afford them or a necessity manufactured under government regulation as needed by this Brave New World.

Before a person can decide whether the law's new status as a religion is a good or bad change, it must be accepted as fact and the nature of the "law" must be understood. The ruling sycophants, hypocrites, and outright cowards who make up the secular bishops and priests of the modern religion that is law have hijacked and claimed as their own the principles and virtues of Christianity's struggles with legal systems of the past. It is the hijacking of these struggles that have given the law whatever sense of justice it has and any credibility it has. The powers-that-be claim that such principles and virtues can be made the norm solely through fear of and intimidation by the law without need of any concept of divine law. This hijacking has been so successful that secular law is now changing the ideology and dogma of Christian churches instead of the other way around.

The nature of this substantive change is difficult to see because of how well the law hides it through the smokescreen of its judge-made law: common law. If five persons wearing military uniforms based on what they consider to be necessary or good for a society at gun point force major alterations of societal relationships and its normative ideology, it would be called a military coup and that government an oligarchy of five tyrants in the Athenian tradition. If five persons put on black judicial robes and force major social change based on what they consider to be necessary or good for that society through their governmental monopoly on violence, it is now considered law simply because they are adept at hiding their personal beliefs and forcing that change behind legal fictions called common law. Such deception only hides the power play, a coup by power-seeking individuals in judicial robes is substantively the same pragmatically as one by military dictators.

The law is marketed by the powers-that-be, and most Americans have accepted as true this marketing of the law, as a system of justice before which all are equal, regardless of whether they are rich or poor. Modern legal systems and cultures are not about justice or about enforcing "law and order" through the "rule of law", the two words "law and order" for all practical purposes in modern legal culture are synonyms and the latter is an illusion: it is about enforcing order through the rule of judges. Order consists of whatever the status quo is in terms of the powers-that-be while equality of power before the law is another illusion. Law now works essentially as a secular religion justifying the ruling class ideology of any given status quo. This reality puts the American legal system on the same rational foundation as the North Korean or any totalitarian legal system. Unlike religion, which for the minority of Americans that regularly practice its rituals is a material concern for daily life only on 1 or 2 days per week, the law of the American legal system is a material concern for all business activity, for all individual public activity, and for a large part of a day's personal activity varying from daily preparation for work, commute to work, workplace-required compliance with a multitude of legal duties and obligations, and then on to the evening news and entertainment that consist in large part of law-related shows.

The law's judges and most of its lawyers are the <u>1984</u> "Outer Party" of modern Technological Society while at the same time acting as a metaphysical Telescreen monitoring all community activity to assure it is compliant with the needs of the "Party". The law's success is founded upon three factors: 1) its oligarchical organizational and structure seeking to maintain the given normative status quo; 2) its unchecked monopoly on the use of violence to enforce its oligarchy and norms; and 3) the constantly moving target smoke screen of "common law" or "case law" (*i.e.*, law made by judges) that hides factors 1 & 2.

This essay is an attempt: 1) to elucidate these factors and to clear the smokescreen to provide an understanding to those not in the Party of the law's workings; 2) if possible, to provide an incentive and a foundation to find alternative ways of thinking about law and the abandoned concept of justice; 3) if alternatives are not possible, to provide an understanding of what the future holds under the rule of judges' arbitrary power; and 4) a guide of how an individual who is not in the Party is to survive while in constant view of the this Telescreen.

So that average citizens will understand the reality of our modern legal culture both in its theory and in practice, this essay will provide a method to understand how to read its private, coded language called case or common law consisting of law made by judges and intentionally written to be as confusing as possible to *hoi polloi* who it considers muggles unworthy of initiation into its secrets. This essay will provide the axioms needed to understand the workings of the common law — by axiom I mean the rules of the game being played. Through methodology and technique, modern society has cured disease, put Man on the Moon, and overcome obstacles that seemed insurmountable only a couple of centuries ago. At the same time, however, modern society's legal culture for dealing with workers are in substance no different than they were 2000 years ago when the goal was to maintain the power elite of the Roman Empire. If a Roman trial lawyer could be taken from the *Basilica Julia*, taught English, and then thrown into a modern courtroom to argue cases for a few weeks, that Roman would be just as competent (or even more competent) than any modern practicing trial lawyer.

Assuming it is possible to do so, to avoid a further progression into a <u>1984</u> legal culture, American workers must re-think their legal culture's dogmatic emphasis on abstract adjudication at the expense of individual justice. Western law is doing dishonestly what most "primitive" legal systems honestly admit to doing: enforcing the ruling class personal morals and social ethics of the judge or judges adjudicating the facts before them — of the judges, not of the juries whose verdicts can be and are routinely overruled when they contradict the morals or ethics of the judge or judges reviewing their verdict. This is a reality that must be changed or accepted as the true reality of the law and then dealt with in order to give substantive meaning to the American form of democracy supposedly founded as a better means of government than a state embodying the idea and leadership of dictatorship or oligarchy.

If it cannot be changed, then we must accept this reality and deal with its ramifications and not continue a delusional belief in American common law as a undisputable good. If America is an oligarchy or a tyranny by a few, for human society to further develop and succeed, workers must accept this and the social ramifications of it. Despite its marketing claiming the opposite purpose and effect, American law does not accept diversity of opinion or personality. It expects 1984 conformity to the abstract principles its secular Outer Party disciples of the Party deem necessary for social order either voluntarily through fear of violence or through actual violent force.

I have come to the conclusion that the making of laws is like the making of sausages—the less you know about the process the more you respect the result.

Many unknown and known trial attorneys

II.   NO RESPECT

The ideal that America is a country founded and defined by the rule of secular law, or any law, is the foundation fraud of present American legal culture.

The reality of American culture's respect for the rule of law is that except for the privileged few its citizens traditionally have had no respect for the rule of law. It is only in recent history that the powers-that-be have gone to great expense and trouble to con Americans into believing that the rule of law is their true religion and protector. It is a recent con for our legal system to market itself as the last defense to liberty by referring to civil rights laws, workers' rights laws, and the rights of criminal defendants in the courts of law that were created solely to stop the civil disobedience and outright violent insurrection that was occurring in American society in protest of enforced inequalities in the law. From Socrates and Jesus Christ to the Haymarket Trials and the 19th Century battles against slavery continuing on to all civil rights and workers' rights battles of the 20th Century including the 1960's, the law was always without exception on the wrong side of history. All these notable battles throughout history by individuals against injustice were by outcasts considered criminals at that time because they worked against the "law" of that time. The cowardice of the judges and lawyers of modern law is best exemplified by their intentional and knowing marketing of itself as a defender of liberty based on the blood of the honored dead who fought against its injustices. It is a complete illusion and delusional for a person to ignore all of history in order to believe that the law in the recent past has changed its nature becoming all of a sudden the right side of history instead of unjust as always.

Even now, according to all available recent studies, approximately 30% of American adults have been arrested. "If you find it surprising, you shouldn't," states Shawn D. Bushway, a criminologist at the University at Albany who is empirically studying criminal histories. "There are a lot more people involved with the criminal-justice system than you know. It's a pretty common American experience." America now houses roughly the same number people with criminal records as it does four-year college graduates. Nearly half of black males and almost 40% of white males are arrested by the age 23.

5

The United States has the largest prison population in the world, and the second-highest per-capita incarceration rate (behind Seychelles that in 2014 had a total prison population of 735 out of a population of around 92,000). According to the U.S. Bureau of Justice Statistics, 2,220,300 adults were incarcerated in US federal and state prisons, and county jails in 2013 (1 in 110) in the U.S. resident population. Additionally, 4,751,400 adults in 2013 (1 in 51) were on probation or on parole. In total, 6,899,000 adults were under correctional supervision (probation, parole, jail, or prison) in 2013 – about 2.8% of adults (1 in 35) in the U.S. resident population. The Vera Institute of Justice reported in 2015 that jails throughout the United States have become warehouses for the poor, the mentally ill, and those suffering from addiction as such individuals lack the financial means or mental capacity to post bail. While the United States represents about 4.4% of the world's population, it houses around 22% of the world's prisoners. According to a 2014 Human Rights Watch report, "tough-on-crime" laws adopted since the 1980s have filled U.S. prisons with mostly non-violent offenders with victimless crimes such as drug users and their suppliers. If all arrested Americans were a nation, they would be the world's 18th largest, being larger than Canada, larger than France, and more than three times the size of Australia.

These statistics cover only Americans who were caught. Only a very small portion of crimes are solved. These statistics do not include the routine suburban users of illegal drugs (police and prosecutors concentrate their efforts on imprisoning the urban poor who act as mules and middlemen for the upper class users). Even when dealing with serious crimes such as murder, according to FBI statistics, police in major cities in an average year solve at best 40% of reported murders. Thus, given the average of 10,000 to 14,000 reported murders per year, just from the last twenty years there may be approximately 100,000 murderers roaming the streets and among us who will never be caught.

If it were somehow possible to count all Americans who have committed a crime, all Americans would be felons multiple times over — many without even knowing it. Estimates of the amount of new state and federal regulations made into law each year vary from a minimum of 3000 to as much as 18,000 if all federal, state, and local regulations could be somehow actually tracked — which they cannot because there are too many. There is no way for an individual to keep track of how many laws they are violating on a regular and routine basis — most Americans most likely commit on average three felonies per day without even knowing it.

Without a doubt, any local, state, or federal government can randomly pick any person in its view and if it were to apply sufficient resources to the task, it could criminally prosecute any one of us and achieve a resulting years, if not a lifetime, of imprisonment. The majority of Americans do not realize how simple and easy it would be for them to go from honest citizen to convicted felon; in fact, honesty may be the one characteristic that would most assure a person would suffer injustice in the American justice system: this is the one virtue that no judge or other members of this Outer Party of American culture expect in court nor respect in practice because of the common law's dishonest emphasis on distortion and illusion to hide the personal ethical decisions that are disguised as law.

The present takeover of the world economy by wage slavery is a general example and the trials and then the conviction of former Illinois Governor Rod Blagojevich is a particular example and are warnings to any worker of what the law intends for them — especially for any worker thinking of using politics as a way into the Inner Party of American legal culture.

Political and social leaders since Aristotle and Cicero of the Roman Republic have complained and argued that wage slavery is a much worse form of human indenture than chattel slavery because it negates any social bond of duty and responsibility between workers and employers. It took civil wars to defeat this belief and the laws that supported and maintained it. Now, somehow, through sleight-of-hand, the law has taken credit for freedom from the chattel slavery it created and enforced while at the same time creating and supporting wage slavery that most historians and economists agree is just as bad if not worse to the human condition.

Mr. Blagojevich did and wanted to do what every politician does: appoint his friends and political donors to political patronage jobs and pass bills and other political acts to benefit himself, friends, and donors. If he had just done those things, for example, had he just appointed his largest donor to fill the seat of departing Senator Obama and shut up about it, there would have been no prosecution. Instead, he outright honestly admitted that he wanted to do that. As a result, Mr. Blagojevich, the son of working class refugees from the Balkans who had worked his way to power, went to prison while President Obama who grew up in the etiquette of the powers and the other powers continue to wine, dine, and play golf with the same donors and friends who through such influence benefit from the President's and any politician's policies in the same way all politicians benefit their friends. Blagojevich was prosecuted because he was honest about what he was doing. This is a common problem with the law. Complying with the law and complying with morality, ethics, and almost always honesty are not the same thing and more often than not work against you.

7

While the law is conducting this mass incarceration and placing a sword of Damocles above all workers, due in large part to the protections granted wealth by the American legal system and other legal systems worldwide, legal "theft" consisting of wealth inequality has seen the largest increase since the Great Depression. In the United States, the top wealthiest 1% possesses 40% of the nation's wealth; the bottom 80% own 7%; the richest 1% in the United States now own more additional income than the bottom 90%. The gap between the top 10% and the middle class is over 1,000%; that increases another 1000% for the top 10% of that 1%. A new Oxfam report shows the vast and growing gap between rich and poor with the 62 richest billionaires in the world owning as much wealth as the poorer half (3 billion) of the world's population.

Given the law's favoritism for the most powerful, why does American culture claim such a respect for the "rule of law" and require that all of its military, police, and naturalized citizens take an oath to defend it? Given the constant, routine violations of law by Americans, knowingly or unknowingly, how is it meaningful to say that America is a society governed by the "rule of law" or that Americans are law-abiding citizens with a respect for the rule of law? This question is especially intriguing given our nation's founding (as with many nations) by rebellion — a revolution against an established rule of law. All of our "Founding Fathers" were criminals under British law and many remained so under American law when they continued with their rebellious nature and criminal activities after the revolution they started in order to protect their criminal activities and ill-gotten gains. They were not criminals as slave owners for those that were because slavery was legal. They were criminals because they were all bootleggers, tax evaders, and black marketeers and many were privateers and outright pirates. The British were completely correct in their complaints that the American colonists wanted the protection of the Royal Navy for their legal and illegal trading but did not want to pay for it. The United States was founded by all sorts criminals and rebels and not by any respect for the law — that came afterward when the successful criminals and rebels wanted a means to protect their ill-gotten gains from a new crop of criminals and rebels.

This issue of America's supposed respect for the rule of law gets further confusing if we were to consider the history and development of American law. Once one leaves areas of law dealing strictly with the retention and protection of wealth such as corporate, probate, anti-trust, or patent law, all progress — without substantive exception — in terms of fostering and protecting the U.S. Constitution's goals of "Justice" or the "Blessings of Liberty" resulted from lawless acts. Beginning with the American Revolution and continuing to slavery, it took a civil war, not the progressive development of the common law, to eliminate slavery. Progress in terms of social justice after the Civil War was, again, achieved despite of and in full violent protest against the law and legal culture rather than through it. Even relatively small issues, such as whether 18 year olds could vote, required the Vietnam War and the forced conscription of thousands of 18 year olds to their deaths to achieve.

The reality is that this "rule of law" stuff is just lawyers' false advertizing and marketing for business purposes. Americans by culture and tradition are not a law-abiding nation — North Korea, Nazi Germany, and Saudi Arabia are law abiding nations by culture and religion. Until recent American history, the American working class and most of middle class culture respected the law when it served their purpose. If it did not serve their purpose, they only complied with the law — but did not necessarily respect it — when their only other option was having an officer of the law forcibly fine them a significant amount of money or imprison them with no way to fight them.

The only Americans in history who always have had an absolute respect for the rule of law were and are its powers-that-be and those attorneys who serve them. This is because the rule of law was always in the powers' favor, even when it appeared to cause them some nominal harm.

As I will discuss later in this essay, in the present reality of the law as a secular religion, having little or no respect for it is not an evil but a good — unless of course you are one of the rich or their priest lawyers and judges. Analytically, empirically, and morally, such disrespect is morally good regardless of how ethics may regard it because it is the only way to challenge any unjust but legal status quo. The modern legal system, unlike ancient tyrants, has no incentive to change because thanks to technology it has a complete monopoly on violence and need not fear the community. It is a tyrant that no longer need fear a Sword of Damocles.

It is not wisdom but authority that makes a law.

Thomas Hobbes

III.   THE FIRST TWO AXIOMS OF THE COMMON LAW

Primitive law lacking the sophistication of modern civilization emphasizes and expects of its government — usually consisting of a religious ruler or a ruling group of religious elders because there was no separation between law, government, and religion — wisdom and justice. In primitive legal systems, the law is seen as a subset of the society's religion. Even for the sophisticated Romans, the five virtues of a Roman citizen were *gravitas*, *pietas*, *dignitas*, and *virtus*. The worship of the gods and the state were unavoidably entwined. Such is exemplified by the first ever major, published case law in legal jurisprudence consisting of King Solomon's adjudication of a child custody case.

One day two women came to King Solomon, and one of them said:

Your Majesty, this woman and I live in the same house. Not long ago my baby was born at home, and three days later her baby was born. Nobody else was there with us.

One night while we were all asleep, she rolled over on her baby, and he died. Then while I was still asleep, she got up and took my son out of my bed. She put him in her bed, then she put her dead baby next to me.

In the morning when I got up to feed my son, I saw that he was dead. But when I looked at him in the light, I knew he wasn't my son.

"No!" the other woman shouted. "He was your son. My baby is alive!"

"The dead baby is yours," the first woman yelled. "Mine is alive!"

They argued back and forth in front of Solomon, until finally he said, "Both of you say this live baby is yours. Someone bring me a sword."

10

A sword was brought, and Solomon ordered, "Cut the baby in half! That way each of you can have part of him."

"Please don't kill my son," the baby's mother screamed. "Your Majesty, I love him very much, but give him to her. Just don't kill him."

The other woman shouted, "Go ahead and cut him in half. Then neither of us will have the baby."

Solomon said, "Don't kill the baby." Then he pointed to the first woman, "She is his real mother. Give the baby to her."

Everyone in Israel was amazed when they heard how Solomon had made his decision. They realized that God had given him wisdom to judge fairly.

1 Kings 3:16-28 Contemporary English Version.

Until the development of DNA testing, modern jurisprudence — despite its millions of pages of law review and case law pontificating on evidence, due process, and the majesty of the law — in any similar case as faced King Solomon most likely would have done no better if not worse. Since there were no witnesses and no physical evidence (prior to DNA), a trial before a judge or jury to resolve the issues presented would have involved the women's testimony and then a final summation in which the baby would be shown to the jury or judge by the trial counsel who would argue the obvious similarity between the baby and their respective client and thus that the baby obviously must be their client's child. In such a trial, as any experienced trial attorney would tell you, you might as well have flipped a coin to decide the result.

Thus, in 3000 years, before the magic of the statistical probability of DNA, jurisprudence made no progress on child custody issues except for adding the phrase "trying to split the baby" into its arguments. Unlike King Solomon's court, modern law still does not have the ability quickly to change a decision once its adverse consequences become obvious.

Even in this first published case law, there appear the first two universal rules or axioms for interpreting judge made law that are sound to this day and for the foreseeable future: 1) the facts given by the judge for a decision have little if anything to do with the actual facts for the decision; and 2) the reasoning given by the judge for the decision has little if anything to do with the actual reasons for the decision. In essence, there is an overriding and dominant "observer effect" in the law in the same way that there is one in the physical sciences only more so. The judge changes the facts and reasoning to achieve a given ethical goal based on the judge's morality and experience. At least in the physical sciences, one can usually quantify and thus pragmatically study any such observer effects. In the law, one cannot. The judge's decision is law, it does not want nor allow for those before it to examine it for error except through the law. Essentially, the logic is as follows: the law is the law unless the law says it is not in which case that is the law. The law is well aware of the tautological nature of this logic but does not care. A lay person reader of case law must be aware of these two axioms when reading and interpreting case law.

The obvious problem with ancient adjudication relying solely on the God-given wisdom of the judge hearing the case is that God gives very few judges the wisdom of a King Solomon. This is especially true of our modern Technological Society in which judges are now political appointees of the secular powers-that-be who spend their entire pre-judge career if not their life brown-nosing to get a judicial appointment so that they do not have to work for a living. A King Solomon in modern judicial ranks is likely an extinct creature.

Civilized society early in its history began the search for an objective determination of justice not relying solely on the wisdom of the judge but on some type of process. Some of these alternatives consisted of Greek and Roman legal systems relying on due process and rhetoric and then as these empires fell — in part due to their failed legal systems — communities tried alternatives such as trial by ordeal, trial by combat, trial by fire, and such other means in which the objective nature of the Almighty was to be the omnipotent adjudicator of the facts. Such "trials" or "ordeals" as an objective basis for adjudication continued to be used in the Western World well into medieval times but had been used in some form going back to the first known codified laws such as the Code of Hammurabi and the Code of Ur-Nammu.

A long historical process then began eliminating trial by ordeal first by the Medieval Church and then by secular governments to be replaced by a preference for ancient Greek and Roman legal procedure but replacing rhetoric with dogma due to the Church's faith in reason (natural law) and divine law as a basis for some justice in life — first in the guise of formal church inquisitions and then in the form of government versions of an inquisition.

With the benefit and arrogance of hindsight and apparently ignorant of our legal culture's foundation in Greek, Roman, and Church Canon Law, modern sycophants of the law from their ivory tower of the farce called law school scholarship ridicule and call past attempts to establish objective systems of justice, especially the inquisition and those based on ordeals, unjust as if they would have done better. It is doubtful that a modern day Thersites, Socrates, or Jesus Christ would succeed any better in our modern legal culture than they did in the ancient world as other writers will discuss later in this essay collection. Recent real scholarly work — not law school polemics — by historians and economists such as Peter Leeson show that these sycophants, as usual, are unjust and factually wrong in their ridicule.

In his empirical study entitled <u>Ordeals</u>, Professor Leeson of George Mason University instead of sitting in his office pontificating about the law and what it should or should not be doing, went out and empirically studied available data on medieval hot iron ordeals in which the judicial process declared parties innocent or not liable if their bodies did not burn when exposed to hot iron rods. Obviously, all skin should burn when touched by a hot iron and thus all defendants should have been found guilty or liable. Instead, after examining the outcomes of a recorded 208 cases in which defendants underwent ordeals, defendants were burned in only 78 cases or 37.5 % of the time. Defendants passed their ordeals in 130 cases or 62.5 % of the time. Unless nearly two-thirds of ordeal-officiating priests did not understand how to heat iron, the only inference that makes sense is that the priests were rigging the results to exculpate defendants. According to Professor Lesson, in the absence of witnesses and physical evidence, the trial by ordeal was effective at sorting the guilty from the innocent because only the truly innocent would choose to endure such a trial; guilty defendants would confess or settle cases instead.

The fairly well-educated priests, well educated relative to their congregation, would be aware of such reality and thus when acting as a judge would routinely rig ordeals so that the participants who they believed innocent could pass them. Princeton history professor Peter Brown explained in his book <u>Society and the Supernatural: A Medieval Change</u> that the ordeal served as a "controlled miracle" within small communities stuck in the social chaos of the Middle Ages that helped avoid feuds and physical fighting and established a social bond among its members in the absence of any higher authority such as a nation state government.

Similarly, modern scholarship by historians, if law professors or law students would bother to read it, has revealed that Church inquisitions had better and fairer procedures and were run with more honesty and concern for objective evidence and mercy for any accused before them than were most secular courts at the time. The Inquisition as a system of justice by a Church that crossed all European borders was originally a welcomed institution to bring "law and order" to Europe because of the chaotic nature and constant feuding among whatever states existed at the time. Though the Inquisition was responsible for approximately 100 witch-hunt deaths, it was also the first judicial body to denounce such trials in Europe. Modern law schools seem to forget that to be educated in Medieval times and during the Renaissance either in the law or in anything usually meant one was educated by a Church institution. Though law school professors continually preach of the Magna Carta as the foundation of modern "rule of law" constitutional jurisprudence, they all seem to forget that it was Archbishop Stephen Langton of the Catholic Church who in 1215 incited and gathered the Barons together to create this document in an attempt to force even the King to admit submission to Divine Law.

At present, there is no realistic opposition from any church or any entity to the modern version of tyranny by "rule of law" that is really "rule by judges".

Of course, no doubt many innocents suffered the injustice of guilt and liability and resulting death or ruin for acts they did not commit, but at least the Church jurists believed they had the sacred task of dealing with the salvation of an individual, specific, immortal soul before them protected by divine law and thus took the concept of individual justice in the case before them seriously. They were not concerned solely with generating abstract principles for use by abstract legal entities. They admittedly dealt with moral and ethical issues and judgments and admitted to the human and thus imperfect form of justice they were using. However, they hoped any injustice will be remedied by the divine justice at the Last Judgment. This is an excuse for injustice we do not have.

Thus, based on historical and empirical evidence and not on the pontificating of law professors, ordeals and inquisitions apparently did as good job of resolving disputes so that social order would be maintained as does our modern convoluted legal system, unless you were an innocent skeptic who failed to show the priests enough respect. In which case, these skeptics were burnt in addition to those innocents whom the priests decided for some other unknown reason should be burned. This is similar to the way that a modern police officer or judge would punish those before them who do not respect their authority or for some other unstated reason.

Though the powers of 21st Century Western legal culture abhor religion and any comparison or association with the supposed evils of Western history and by principle try to separate themselves in every way from Western religion and history, the modern legal culture emphasizing reliance upon abstract principles and systematic legal constructs such as corporations, contracts, estates, rights, and legal duties are founded upon and directly result from dogmatic Christian Cannon Law only without the belief and hope in divine justice. Instead, modern law has a religious belief in abstract rules for later use by abstract legal entities that are more important than any individual, such as corporations, with the goal not being justice in the specific case before it — unless there is sympathy for the specific case before it — but the maintenance of a given social order through abstract principles.

The next attempt at progressive evolution of the law caused by the power struggles between the Church and developing nation states was to be the elimination of reliance upon Divine intervention (supposedly acting through priests) and instead to rely purely on the new gods of due process and the rule of law to reach judgments that supposedly truly separated the innocent from the guilty. Or not.

[W]hile the terminology of morals is still retained, and while the law does still and always, in a certain sense, measure legal liability by moral standards, it nevertheless, by the very necessity of its nature, is continually transmuting those moral standards into external or objective ones, from which the actual guilt of the party concerned is wholly eliminated. ... The first requirement of a sound body of law is, that it should correspond with the actual feelings and demands of the community, whether right or wrong. If people would gratify the passion of revenge outside of the law, if the law did not help them, the law has no choice but to satisfy the craving itself, and thus avoid the greater evil of private retribution. ....

The Common Law, Oliver Wendell Holmes Jr.

IV.   THE THIRD AND FOURTH AXIOMS OF THE COMMON LAW

In reality, nothing has changed. Despite pretensions to the contrary, the guilt, innocence, or liability of any individual before a modern court matters no more and probably less now than it did in the medieval ordeals or before a medieval religious or secular inquisition. In those medieval cases, at least the judges believed they had the sacred task of dealing with the salvation of an individual, specific, and immortal souls before them protected by divine law. Now, the individual is simply a sand pebble in national and multi-national global forces that need the social order — not any individual worker — provided by the law in order to continue and prosper. As with the priests of the Middle Ages, modern judges who are the modern-day priests of the new secular religion called the law decide how and when to rig the results so as to maintain social order by an appearance of justice irrespective of the actual guilt or innocence of the parties and disputes before them and without need of any definition or even concept of justice.

The above-quoted statements by Judge Oliver Wendell Holmes Jr. in his book The Common Law are according to one of the few judges of the American legal system entitled to respect independently of the required respect shown to them as judges. His statements are both definition and condemnation of the American legal system. His book The Common Law should be required reading in every American law school; it is not, with its absence there is also a complete absence of any required reading or study of the history of law — I will later discuss the reasons for this lack of historical study. In a time when historical study and analytic study and thought is becoming less and less important in college and pre-college education, the reading and study of major portions of The Common

Law should be required study at some point in that education in order to prepare the students to live as citizens under the power of the law. It is not so required and will not be required any time in the foreseeable future.

The unique life and experience of a Justice Holmes allowed him to reveal in his book the workings of the inner sanctum of American legal culture. Unlike the present prophets of American Legal Culture varying from the likes of Lawrence Tribe and Richard Allen Posner to all of the Supremes on the United States Supreme Court who essentially have gone through life in protected bubbles immune from any uncontrolled dangers or even minor insecurities in their lives that were spent concerned wholly with their professional careers, Justice Holmes experienced the ultimate evil and good of human nature: war.

At the outset of the American Civil War, Holmes enlisted in the Massachusetts militia and received a commission as first lieutenant in the Massachusetts Volunteer Infantry. He saw combat action varying from the Peninsula Campaign to the Wilderness, suffering wounds at the Battle of Ball's Bluff, Antietam, and Chancellorsville, and almost died from dysentery. Holmes eventually rose to the rank of lieutenant colonel while seeing many of the friends who joined with him die along the way. Legend has it that while a captain at the Battle of Fort Stevens, Justice Holmes shouted at then President Abraham Lincoln standing out in the line with his 6-foot-4 inch frame plus frock coat and top hat observing that battle close to its front lines as he often did during the Civil War: "Get down, you damn fool!". (He always stated that it was someone else.)

He personally experienced the random nature of life and death in war and thus knew clearly and undisputedly that fate took the guilty and innocent alike. It is not surprising then that he eventually concludes that if there is any rationality in the term "justice", it was created by human law and not by any divine law. Unlike the vast majority of judges and law professors both at that time and since, Holmes actually practiced law before becoming a law professor and judge. His major scholarly work, The Common Law, remains the only accepted major scholarly work written by a practicing attorney and most likely will remain so for the foreseeable future because even at present practicing law is considered to be a hindrance and disadvantage for supposed scholarly work in the law. Every American citizen as part of their education should at a minimum read the opening paragraphs of the Common Law:

> The life of the law has not been logic; it has been experience. The felt necessities of the time, the prevalent moral and political theories, intuitions of public policy, avowed or unconscious, and even the prejudices which

17

judges share with their fellow-men, have had a good deal more to do than syllogism in determining the rules by which men should be governed. The law embodies the story of a nation's development through many centuries, and it cannot be dealt with as if it contained only the axioms and corollaries of a book of mathematics.

In his book, Holmes set forth his view that the only source of law was a judicial decision enforced by the state. Judges decided cases on the facts as they saw them and then wrote opinions afterward that presented a rationale for their decision. The true basis of the decision was often an "inarticulate major premise." However, almost always, a judge was obliged to choose between opposing and contradictory but equally rational legal arguments and the true basis of his decision was sometimes drawn from outside the law.

According to Judge Holmes and all modern polemics on the law without exception, including among so-called "liberal" judges that claim to respect rights of the minority against any tyranny by a majority, though each individual in theory has a right to pursuit their own happiness, the happiness of any individual is irrelevant and can be sacrificed to assure the social order of the whole. Thus, human "progress" in jurisprudence has consisted of going from trying to avoid the injustice of reliance on the wisdom of a King Solomon for achieving justice and truth for the individuals before the court to giving up on any hope for justice and truth, accepting instead the rule of law defined as social order as its substitute.

However, neither Judge Holmes nor modern versions of his pragmatic views go far enough because he saw and all modern legal culture sees the law from the perspective of the powers-that-be. It must not be forgotten that it was Judge Holmes who wrote the decision in Buck v. Bell, 274 U.S. 200 (1927) in which the Court ruled that a state statute permitting compulsory sterilization of those the state considers unfit, including those alleged to be intellectually disabled "for the protection and health of the state", did not violate the Due Process clause of the Fourteenth Amendment to the United States Constitution. Not only does this decision stand as good law, as most recently cited by the federal 8th Circuit Court of Appeals in 2001, but it made good argument and fodder at the Nuremberg trials by defense counsel for the Nazis accused as war criminals for advocating and carrying out the exact same law. It appears that Holmes' witnessing of the random violence and death of war made him a pragmatist on the law as well as on ethics and morals as would be expected of an officer and a gentleman required to do his duty to shoot the wounded and deserters and to carry out other forms of decimation as needed.

A modified version of Judge Holmes' "first requirement of a sound body of law" is the third axiom for reading and interpreting common law: any given body of law will correspond with the actual feelings and demands of the community's ruling class ideology regardless of whether it is morally right or wrong.

The fourth and final axiom of case law can be concerned a corollary of the third axiom: any law, regardless of first effect or appearance, will eventually become a means for the ruling class to maintain its power.

These final axioms give meaning and purpose to the law as the "Outer Party" of our modern, sophisticated version of a 1984 society.

Thus, the four axioms for reading and interpreting case or common law are:

1) the facts given by the judge for a decision have little if anything to do with the actual facts for the decision;

2) the reasoning given by the judge for the decision has little if anything to do with the actual reasons for the decision;

3) any given body of law will correspond with the actual feelings and demands of the community's ruling class ideology regardless of whether it is morally right or wrong;

4) any law, regardless of first effect or appearance, will eventually become a means for the ruling class to maintain its power.

These axioms must be understood as working with the law's: 1) oligarchical organizational and normative structure; and 2) its unchecked monopoly on the use of violence to enforce its oligarchy and norms.

Though the law talks of equality and diversity, there is probably no area of modern American culture that is more explicitly made up of an oligarchy of power than legal culture. Every aspect of legal culture from solo practitioners to associates to partners, from appointed defense counsel to millionaire defense counsel, from low level district court judges to high level appellate judges, and from lawyers to "overseers" is made up of firmly established oligarchies of power.

The law is the only area of modern society that is allowed to practice unrestricted violence upon others for enforcement of its oligarchy — the only restriction is the law restricting itself if it wants.

Welcome to the real world.   Morphesus, The Matrix

Young man, let me remind you that this is a court of law and not a court of justice.
Judge Oliver Wendell Holmes Jr., U.S. Supreme Court, during an oral
argument

V. THE PARTY

Any examination or reading of American and world history would establish
that law, especially the common law that can be changed by individual judges on a
daily basis, does not evolve because civilized society and judges evolve together
by "continually transmuting ... moral standards into external or objective ones" and
then into laws — but this occurs by transmuting the specific individual moral
standards of the judge or the ethics of a society's ruling class into law: the law is
one and the same as ruling class ideology. Law professors try to make a distinction
between "rule by law" in which the ruling class is specifically exempted from any
law that they give or enforce and "rule of law" as supposedly a better way, in
which the ruling class is also subject to the law's monopoly on violence. This
distinction is substantively meaningless as is most falsely entitled law school
"scholarship." Furthermore, in modern culture, as any scholarly analysis of
common law would show, the "rule of law" and "rule by judges" is also
substantively the same and "law and order" is the same as "order."

The common law jumps around as the modern ruling class jumps around and
changes its membership, its ethics, and its morals as necessary to reflect and to
counter any threats to this power from non-members of the ruling class. As a much
better writer than me has already stated:

> As compared with their opposite numbers in past ages, the new aristocracy
> was less avaricious, less tempted by luxury, hungrier for pure power, and,
> above all, more conscious of what they were doing and more intent on
> crushing opposition. This last difference was cardinal. By comparison with
> that existing today, all the tyrannies of the past were half-hearted and
> inefficient. The ruling groups were always infected to some extent by liberal
> ideas, and were content to leave loose ends everywhere, to regard only the
> overt act, and to be uninterested in what their subjects were thinking. Even
> the Catholic Church of the Middle Ages was tolerant by modern standards.
> Part of the reason for this was that in the past no government had the power
> to keep its citizens under constant surveillance. The invention of print,
> however, made it easier to manipulate public opinion, and the film and the

20

radio carried the process further. With the development of television and the personal computer, and the technical advances which made it possible to receive and transmit simultaneously on the same instrument, private life came to an end. Every citizen, or at least every citizen important enough to be worth watching, could be kept for twenty-four-hours a day under the eyes of the police and in the sound of official propaganda, with all other channels of information closed. The possibility of enforcing not only complete obedience to the will of the State, but complete uniformity of opinion on all subjects, now existed for the first time.

Nothing the citizen does is indifferent or neutral. His or her friendships, hobbies, behavior towards his or her spouse or lover, facial expressions, gestures, characteristic movements, tones of voice, words muttered while asleep -- all are jealously scrutinized. Not only any actual misdemeanor, but any eccentricity, however small, any change of habits, any nervous mannerism that could possibly be the symptom of an inner struggle, is certain to be detected. Endless purges, arrests, tortures, imprisonments, and disappearances are inflicted both as punishments for crimes which have been actually committed and as the systematic wiping-out of any persons who might perhaps commit a crime at some time in the future.

And so today the determining factor in perpetuating a totally obsolete hierarchical society is the mental attitude of the ruling class itself. The problem, that is to say, is educational. It is a problem of continuously molding the consciousness both of the directing group and of the larger executive group that lies immediately below it. Skepticism and hesitancy among the ranks of the rulers must be prevented. (As will be seen in Chapter 3, the best method of molding consciousness is continuous warfare.)

The consciousness of the masses (the "proles"), by contrast, needs only be influenced in a negative way. The masses could only become dangerous if the advance of industrial technique made it necessary to educate them more highly: but, since military and commercial rivalries are no longer of primary importance, the level of popular education is actually declining. What opinions the masses hold, or do not hold, is looked upon as a matter of indifference. They can be granted intellectual liberty because it is thought that they have no intellect. In a member of the ruling elite, on the other hand, not even the smallest deviation of opinion on the most unimportant subject can be tolerated.

All the beliefs, habits, tastes, emotions, mental attitudes that characterize our time are really designed to sustain the mystique of the rulers and prevent the true nature of present-day society from being perceived. A member of the elite is required to have not only the right opinions, but the right instincts. Many of the beliefs and attitudes demanded of him or her are never plainly stated, and could not be stated without laying bare the contradiction at the heart of modern-day hierarchical society. To maintain this regime, a continuous alteration of the past is necessary. Both the elites and the masses will tolerate present-day conditions because they have no standards of comparison. Everyone must be cut off from the past, as well as from other countries, because it is necessary for one and all to believe that everyone is better off than his or her ancestors and that the average level of material comfort is rising. But by far the most important reason for the constant readjustment of the past is to safeguard the validity of the system itself. It is not merely that speeches, statistics, and records of every kind can and must be constantly brought up to date in order to show that the fundamental principles of society are sound. No change in these basic principles -- work, commodity production, private property, the State -- can ever be admitted. For to change one's mind is a confession of weakness, and weakness cannot be tolerated in a "perfect" system.

...

From the point of view of our present rulers, therefore, the only genuine dangers are the splitting-off of a new group of able, under-employed, power-hungry people, and the growth of liberalism and scepticism in their own ranks. The problem, that is to say, is educational. It is a problem of continuously moulding the consciousness both of the directing group and of the larger executive group that lies immediately below it. The consciousness of the masses needs only to be influenced in a negative way.

In principle, membership [in the Party] is not hereditary. The child of Inner Party parents is in theory not born into the Inner Party. ... . Nor is there any racial discrimination, or any marked domination of one province by another. Jews, Negroes, South Americans of pure Indian blood are to be found in the highest ranks of the Party, and the administrators of any area are always drawn from the inhabitants of that area. ... Its rulers are not held together by blood-ties but by adherence to a common doctrine. It is true that our society is stratified, and very rigidly stratified, on what at first sight appear to be hereditary lines. There is far less to-and-fro movement between the different groups than happened under capitalism or even in the pre-industrial age. Between the two branches of the Party there is a certain amount of interchange, but only so much as will ensure that weaklings are excluded from the Inner Party and that ambitious members of the Outer Party are made harmless by allowing them to rise. Proletarians, in practice, are not allowed to graduate into the Party. The most gifted among them, who might possibly become nuclei of discontent, are simply marked down by the Thought Police and eliminated. But this state of affairs is not necessarily permanent, nor is it a matter of principle. The Party is not a class in the old sense of the word. It does not aim at transmitting power to its own children, as such; and if there were no other way of keeping the ablest people at the top, it would be perfectly prepared to recruit an entire new generation from the ranks of the proletariat. In the crucial years, the fact that the Party was not a hereditary body did a great deal to neutralize opposition. The older kind of Socialist, who had been trained to fight against something called 'class privilege' assumed that what is not hereditary cannot be permanent. He did not see that the continuity of an oligarchy need not be physical, nor did he pause to reflect that hereditary aristocracies have always been shortlived, whereas adoptive organizations such as the Catholic Church have sometimes lasted for hundreds or thousands of years. The essence of oligarchical rule is not father-to-son inheritance, but the persistence of a certain world-view and a certain way of life, imposed by the dead upon the living. A ruling group is a ruling group so long as it can nominate its successors. The Party is not concerned with perpetuating its blood but with perpetuating itself. Who wields power is not important, provided that the hierarchical structure remains always the same.

All the beliefs, habits, tastes, emotions, mental attitudes that characterize our time are really designed to sustain the mystique of the Party and prevent the true nature of present-day society from being perceived. Physical rebellion, or any preliminary move towards rebellion, is at present not possible. From the proletarians nothing is to be feared. Left to themselves, they will continue from generation to generation and from century to century, working, breeding, and dying, not only without any impulse to rebel, but without the power of grasping that the world could be other than it is. They could only become dangerous if the advance of industrial technique made it necessary to educate them more highly; but, since military and commercial rivalry are no longer important, the level of popular education is actually declining. What opinions the masses hold, or do not hold, is looked on as a matter of indifference. They can be granted intellectual liberty because they have no intellect. In a Party member, on the other hand, not even the smallest deviation of opinion on the most unimportant subject can be tolerated.

1984, George Orwell.

The reasons for this universal tyranny of the Party is unclear and most likely will always be unclear because no one is studying it and soon no one will be allowed to study it. However, the reasons may be quite simple. First, the individual dies, but the individual's social group if properly maintained does not. As specifically said by Adolf Hitler but implicitly believed by all powers from the lowest Marine Corps sergeant to the greatest of conquerors: "What is life? Life is the nation. The individual must die anyway. Beyond the life of the individual is the nation." Second, whenever one person by skill, ambition, or by luck is able to work their way from prol to Party member, they are no longer a prol but a Party member and thus, given the selfishness of human nature, no longer cares nor thinks like a prol. Such is not true of race, ethnicity, sex, nor any other classification one uses for humans. If a person of a certain race or ethnicity goes from prol to Party member, they remain that race or ethnicity. Thus the Party is the holy grail of modern law as the great universal equalizer of all races, sexes, ethnicities, and whatever — of all except for economic and thus political class.

Though Judge Holmes' life experience gave him a unique incentive and perspective to reveal the inner workings of the Party, it must be remembered that Judge Holmes also was without doubt a member of America's ruling class and saw the world from its perspective — he was not only a member of the Outer Party but also a member of the Inner Party whose self-confidence and unique life experience allowed him to reveal some of its inner workings without fear of being kicked out or of destroying its power. He saw war through the eyes of a commissioned officer and not that of a conscripted or enlisted common soldier. Thus, even in war and his eye-witnessing of its randomness, he had a controlled empowered version of reality that was far removed from the completely random life of the common soldier. Regardless, the average citizen can learn much from his revelations about the ruling class' creation of the common law, more than they or anyone can from any modern American study of law. There are at present a group of academics at

24

many law schools who call themselves "philosophers of law" thus insulting both the learning of philosophers and the practice of lawyers. The fact that such remain over one hundred years after Judge Holmes' book is further proof of how backward and antiquated American legal culture is in terms of analytical study of its nature — but then again, it does not care nor need it care as long as it serves the Party's purpose.

Pay no attention to that man behind the curtain.

Wizard of Oz

VI.   THE REALITY OF THE COMMON LAW

The judges and the attorney as bishops and priests of the common law make up a large part of America's Outer Party and also serve as its Telescreen and its Newspeak, providing the process and language that the Party uses to give the illusion of being a system of justice instead of just a system for maintaining order through a monopoly on force and violence. The common law makes our legal system so convoluted, inconsistent, and contradictory that citizens need a lawyer (almost always a member of the Outer Party) if they want any hope of deluding themselves into having deciphered its requirements but even then, after hiring a lawyer, more often than not they are just as confused and still are not able to accurately decipher, understand, or comply with whatever the law may or may not want a citizen to do or not do. So much of law is convoluted and inconsistent — in fact, it sometimes changes on a daily if not hourly basis — and makes no sense either analytically or pragmatically that we essentially live in a lawless society pretending to be governed by the "rule of law". The reality of case law and the common law is that the law is what any particular judge says the it is on any given day as a reflection of whatever the present ruling class ideology is on that day; it is a disguise for enforcement of a particular judge's morals or ethics; and the only rule of evidence is what the judge wants to hear as evidence on any particular day. The best analogy for the American legal culture is a baseball game in which the umpires at each base not only change the rules of the game at each base but do so randomly and arbitrarily so that no player or runner knows the rules until they get to the base and the umpire either rules for or against them — next time around, the rules may change again.

Though only 5% to 10% of attorneys (at most) are involved in the trial and case law or common law portion of the present American legal system, it is this aspect of the law that is the foundation for the credibility of all out-of-court administrative, counsel, and regulatory law; if it were not for the necessity of reading and understanding case law, there would be no need for non-trial lawyers. Anyone can draft and read rules or statutes. Most jobs, vocations, professions, games, and essentially anyone needing rules for something can draft rules for whatever they are doing: engineers draft engineering operating procedures and

26

standards; electricians for their vocation; sailors; soldiers; doctors; tax agents; dog catchers; and so forth. The only reason for getting lawyers involved in the drafting, negotiation, and enforcement of rules and regulations and related resolution of disputes is because they supposedly have special training in understanding the long history and supposed guidance of the common law in resolution of disputes in a just manner (anyone can resolve a dispute in an unjust manner). Since the law has become not a process for justice but simply of order through enforcement of judges' morals and ethics under threat of violence that for workers means being economic slaves to global powers, as I will analyze further in this essay, workers have no reason to continue to trust in any aspect of the law.

For now, I want to immediately analyze some famous Supreme Court decisions to show you how to see through the smokescreen if you honestly concentrate on these given axioms and apply them to case law along with life experience and readily available history. In doing so, one must ignore the 100 years of bullshit that the powerful and their attorneys with the aid of their anointed judges have spent generating as a smokescreen to their movements and think clearly, through reason and life experience, about case law.

A. Plessy v. Ferguson, 163 U.S. 537 (1896)

The first case is Plessy v. Ferguson, 163 U.S. 537 (1896). This is a much-maligned case, as it should be, by present law school sycophants though, again, this is purely polemic and without any reference either to history or to its substance. This case is important because it shows the axioms of the common law at work. Furthermore, by comparing it to more recent case law, you can see how the power of the common law has become almost completely independent of any residue or remaining concerns for community ethics or morality as a basis for maintaining social order and instead has moved to complete reliance on the ethics and morality of the minority that make up the powers-that-be or Inner Party of our society without any improvement either in American society overall, either economically or culturally, or in the life of the working or middle class.

The entire Plessy case is now as with most case law readily available on the internet. However, as the first two axioms state, reading it to gain a clear understanding as to the basis and reasoning for its conclusions is a waste of time — even for a relatively simple case such as this written in relatively concise and direct wording that could be understood even by the uninitiated. However, at least anyone with reasonable intelligence can read Plessy and make sense of its reasoning, something that would not be true of even the simplest of common law today. It was written in simpler times when American common law published decisions could probably be contained in a personal office bookstand instead of requiring an entire library as is the situation now. At one point this decision actually admits to the ethical basis for its conclusion that could have just as easily gone the other way if a majority of the judges wanted to go the other way, unlike now in which such honesty would be impossible in any judicial decision:

> We consider the underlying fallacy of the plaintiff's argument to consist in the assumption that the enforced separation of the two races stamps the colored race with a badge of inferiority. If this be so, it is not by reason of anything found in the act, but solely because the colored race chooses to put that construction upon it. The argument necessarily assumes that if, as has been more than once the case and is not unlikely to be so again, the colored race should become the dominant power in the state legislature, and should enact a law in precisely similar terms, it would thereby relegate the white race to an inferior position. We imagine that the white race, at least, would not acquiesce in this assumption. The argument also assumes that social prejudices may be overcome by legislation, and that equal rights cannot be secured to the negro except by an enforced commingling of the two races. We cannot accept this proposition. If the two races are to meet upon terms of social equality, it must be the result of natural affinities, a mutual appreciation of each other's merits, and a voluntary consent of individuals. As was said by the Court of Appeals of New York in People v. Gallagher, 93 N. Y. 438, 448, this end can neither be accomplished nor promoted by laws which conflict with the general sentiment of the community upon whom they are designed to operate. When the government, therefore, has secured to each of its citizens equal rights before the law and equal opportunities for improvement and progress, it has accomplished the end for which it was organized, and performed all of the functions respecting social advantages with which it is endowed.

Legislation is powerless to eradicate racial instincts or to abolish distinctions based upon physical differences, and the attempt to do so can only result in accentuating the difficulties of the present situation. If the civil and political rights of both races be equal, one cannot be inferior to the other civilly or politically. If one race be inferior to the other socially, the Constitution of the United States cannot put them upon the same plane.

Though this decision is much misaligned these days as part of the politically correct speech that makes up law school "scholarship", Plessy has never been formally vacated or reversed by the Supreme Court and can in fact be cited as law if the situation ever arises for such citation. In 1952, Attorney William H. Rehnquist, then a law clerk to Justice Robert H. Jackson, prepared a memorandum called "A Random Thought on the Segregation Cases" urging Justice Jackson to reject arguments made by lawyers in Brown v. Board of Education, another landmark segregation case, and to uphold Plessy. Rehnquist wrote, "I realize that this is an unpopular and unhumanitarian position for which I have been excoriated by 'liberal' colleagues, but I think Plessy v. Ferguson was right and should be re-affirmed." He continued, "To the argument… that a majority may not deprive a minority of its constitutional right, the answer must be made that while this is sound in theory, in the long run it is the majority who will determine what the constitutional rights of the minority are." Of course, when Rehnquist came up before the Senate for confirmation to the Supreme Court, with the integrity (or lack thereof) shown by most nominees, he denied that this memo was his opinion and tried to pass the buck to the dead judge for whom he had been working.

As is usually the case, pursuing the first two axioms, the real facts and reasoning behind the Plessy decision are much more fascinating and intellectually challenging than the common law smokescreen written into the decision to hide them. Because the decision was issued over a hundred years ago, luckily we have the work of historian and non-law school scholars by which to read and interpret it. If Judge Henry Billings Brown, who wrote the majority decision in Plessy, had been forced to write reality and ethics instead of being forced by legal culture to hide both behind the smokescreen of the common law, both at its issuance and now, we would really have some interesting intellectual issues to discuss that could involve most Americans and be understood by most, not just those initiated or deluded into the Outer Party. Such honest discussion might have avoided or at least lessened the over a century's worth of Jim Crow laws that it caused. The historical facts that are the basis for the ethical decision that is Plessy viewed through the majority's personal morals and ethics and not its cited law, facts, or logic could have easily gone the other way if the judges wanted to rule any other way. These facts are as follows.

Plessy was issued in 1896. The Civil War had ended <50 years earlier. Both its memory and effects were still active social forces and, unlike World War I and II for the baby boom and succeeding generations, this memory and effects were not primarily good ones about fighting a noble war against evil and America becoming a world power. About 625,000 men died in the Civil War. That is more Americans than died in both World Wars, Korea, and Vietnam combined. These deaths amounted to 2% of the entire population at the time, which would be the equivalent to about 6 million Americans males dying in a war today. Think about what social trauma American society would have now in 2016 if 6 million American males had died 50 years ago during the Vietnam War.

What was the economic impact of the Civil War on American life? It was the most expensive undertaking by the federal government before or since in relative terms. In 1860 the federal budget was $63 million and the national debt was $65 million. We had limited government, a small federal budget, and low taxes. In 1860, on the eve of war, almost all federal revenue derived from import and export tariffs. We had no income tax, no estate tax, and no excise taxes. Even the whiskey tax and the small revolution it caused were gone. Four years of civil war changed all that forever. In 1865 the national debt stood at $2.7 billion with the annual interest on that debt being twice our entire national budget in 1860. After the war, annual budgets regularly exceeded $300 million. The United States passed a progressive income tax, an estate tax, and excise taxes to pay off that debt. The South was in financial ruin both financially and structurally and remained so until well into the 20th Century. Federal pensions to Union veterans became one of the largest items in the federal budget (except for the interest payment on the Civil War debt itself). By 1896, the Americans lived through both the Long Depression of 1873–79 and the following Panic of 1893.

Though General Lee of the Confederacy surrendered to Union General Grant on 9 April 1865, technically that was not the end of the Civil War. Because of continuing "insurrection" in parts of the South, President Johnson did not declare an end to the Civil War until August 20, 1866. It was somewhat of a miracle that the "insurrection" did not continue by para-military forces for decades if not longer as usually occurs in civil wars that have been fought throughout the world. The Second Amendment at that time was not just a symbol as it is now. Groups could have, as often occurred during and after the civil war, create paramilitary militia that fought and caused physical and social harm throughout the North and South long after the Civil War preventing any type of meaningful "union" of the two or of a viable nation state. Think of the tortured history of the Balkans for example.

It was into this social fabric that the staged case of Plessy v. Ferguson was intentionally created by a small group of individuals who naively ignored the above four axioms of the common law.

In 1890, the state of Louisiana passed the Separate Car Act requiring separate accommodations for blacks and whites on railroads, including separate railway cars. A group of prominent black, creole, and white New Orleans residents called the Comité des Citoyens (Committee of Citizens) decided to fight. The Committee could have fought it in the way that such fights were usually fought through history and that were fought by the post-World War II civil rights movement: either by armed conflict or by economic conflict. Armed protest or conflict then was viable — such is no longer a viable option given the strength of the modern state and its well paid and well armed mercenary police forces. However, economic conflict was also a very viable option. The railroads opposed the Act because it burdened them with the expense of additional railroad cars. It would have been a very viable option for the Committee to return the favor to the white supremacists who passed the Act by boycotting the railroad and any businesses owed by them and thus to gather further support from the powerful railroad interests.

Instead, the Committee made a mistake that has become the mistake of most modern America protest continually to this day, especially by the leaders of the Black American civil rights movement: it put its faith in the "law." Such faith was and continues to be their weakness. By appealing to the "law" as its protector and asking judges and lawyers to take risks that its members were too cowardly to take, it not only empowered the law but at the same time made itself appear inferior to all those other groups varying from Chinese immigrants or communist unionists who were willing to make economic and personal risks to achieve justice. The Committee was not willing to risk economic harm to its interests nor personal harm to its members by engaging in boycotts or civil disobedience protests against the white supremacists who passed the Act but somehow expected the law to accept and make such risks for society — a fact no doubt noted by the judges before whom the Committee's attorneys appeared, though this fact was never explicitly stated in the decisions as would be expected by the axioms.

On the surface, ignoring the above axioms, the Committee appeared to be justified in relying that the law would save the day given the details of its setup. It persuaded Homer Plessy, a man of mixed race, to participate in an orchestrated test case. Plessy was born a free man and was an "octoroon" (of seven-eighths European descent and one-eighth African descent). Thus, if he had not said anything, he could have "passed" as a white man as many others did and ridden in the white person's car. However, under Louisiana law, he was classified as black, and thus required to sit in the "colored" car. This detail shows the irrational and practical absurdity of the law and its irrational foundation in racism.

On June 7, 1892, Plessy bought a first-class ticket and boarded a "whites only" car of the East Louisiana Railroad in New Orleans, Louisiana, bound for Covington, Louisiana. Not only had the Committee previously told the railroad company of Plessy's racial lineage and his intent to challenge the law, the Committee hired a private detective with arrest powers to detain Plessy to assure he was charged for violating the Separate Car Act instead of some other law such as trespass or disorderly conduct. After Plessy took a seat in the whites-only railway car, the arrest occurred and the judicial process began. It moved all the way up to the United States Supreme Court as the Committee intended.

Long before this setup in 1868, the United States Constitution had been amended via the 14th Amendment stating:

> All persons born or naturalized in the United States, and subject to the jurisdiction thereof, are citizens of the United States and of the State wherein they reside. No State shall make or enforce any law which shall abridge the privileges or immunities of citizens of the United States; nor shall any State deprive any person of life, liberty, or property, without due process of law; nor deny to any person within its jurisdiction the equal protection of the laws.

So, based on a straightforward reading of the above Due Process clause and based on the straightforward facts of a physically white person arrested for trying to ride in a white person's car because of a law written by racists for a purely irrational racist purpose despite the fighting of the Civil War to stop such nonsense, the Committee appeared to have the facts, the law, and logic on its side and thus a sure winner, right? In addition, it had one of the major ideals on its side that led to the Civil War in the first place: abolition of slavery? Not.

The Committee made the mistake of believing that the law made decisions based on the facts, law, and logic before it — that based on the facts before it that the law seeks a rational concept of justice. It does no such thing. It seeks to maintain social order based on what the morality and ethics of its judges — regardless of the facts, logic, or written law or logical reasoning before them.

For Mr. Plessy to have won, a majority of the Supremes deciding Plessy would have had to possess a personal factual background and personal morality that would lead them to believe that instead of accepting the status quo of active racism in the law, ethics instead required that: 1) they risk social order and the start of another insurrection to achieve individual justice for the individual Plessy, or 2) risk concrete social order and another actual insurrection by enforcing the abstract principles for which the last insurrection was fought instead of the abstract principles that would maintain the present status quo social order. So, who were these King Solomon's who would make the choice of ethics?

Judge Brown who wrote the majority decision in <u>Plessy</u> would fit well into any judiciary of any country, of any political nature, of any time, including our American 21st Century. He came from an upper-class merchant family who paid for his attendance at both Harvard and Yale. After the usual upper class year long tour of Europe that indoctrinated him into the universal nature of his economic class, he went on to practice admiralty law in Michigan (dealing with shipping on the Great Lakes). At times he served as a government prosecutor. He did not serve in the Union Army during the Civil War but like many rich men instead hired a substitute soldier to take his place. It is unknown what happened to that poor soul. So, he was a coward. After he married and the death of his father-in-law left him independently wealthy, he decided in the finest traditions of his class to take a cut in pay to become a judge eventually kissing his way up to the Supremes. He was a man, lawyer, judge, and citizen that could be counted on to follow orders and do what he was told decisively and steadfastly. He was the kind of man upon whose shoulders empires are run and maintained (though not built) — regardless of their political nature. He would be as comfortable in Nazi Germany as he was in the United States — as long as there was social order and everyone knew their place, he would fit in. No way would he risk anything for Mr. Plessy.

The Chief Judges Melville Fuller, Horace Gray, George Shiras, Jr., Edward D. White, and Peckham were no better. Fuller came from a family of Maine lawyers and simply decided to continue the family tradition in Chicago, Illinois where he spent the Civil War years avoiding military service and in Illinois government positions as a Democratic making life difficult for the Republican President Lincoln. Grey was an old guard New England Yankee who spent his whole life, except for a tour of Europe as required for the youth of his class, in Massachusetts as a glorified bookkeeper churning out decisions for the Massachusetts Supremes and then for the U.S. Supremes. Shiras was an attorney for the rich and powerful his whole life before his family and corporate connections made him a Supreme. Peckham came from an old guard upper New York family of lawyers who as a friend of all wealthy spent his whole life passing judgment on others' lives from the comfort of his office. The idea that these men would risk anything for anybody was ludicrous. White was a former Confederate Army officer: whatever risks he was winning to take were without a doubt not on behalf of the likes of Mr. Plessy or his cause. Thus, a majority of the Court would, regardless of the facts, law, or reasoning before it, rule against Mr. Plessy.

Justice Brewer, the one other judge who had a history of voting for equal rights for blacks despite his sheltered background, was away attending to a family illness when the <u>Plessy</u> case was heard. Judge Stephen Field was somewhat of an aberration. Though he came from an old-guard New England Yankee family, he practiced law in California mining and wilderness areas, usually carrying two guns to protect himself and believing in dueling to defend his honor. He was specifically appointed to the Supreme Court to a newly created 10th seat during the Civil War to change its ideology and thus its rulings. He supported equality for Chinese people while a judge in California but consistently ruled against any equality for blacks so he may have been a racist and thus could not be expected to help out Mr. Plessy — he did not but might have. Regardless, these two would have been in the minority even with the addition of Judge Harlan, so Mr. Plessy still would have lost.

Judge John M. Harlan was another aberration. Born into a prominent family in Kentucky that owed slaves, he was pro-union but a supporter of slavery. He was in the Union Army for a portion of the Civil War until required to leave because of the death of his father to manage the family estate. He had a half-brother that was mulatto apparently the child of his father and a slave. He is known as the great dissenter in <u>Plessy</u>. Given his stated bigotry against the Chinese as even admitted in his <u>Plessy</u> dissent, how much of that dissent is due to his guilty conscience over his half-brother and his family's slave ownership will never be know because, again, the common law did not allow him to honestly discuss these factors in his decision. Instead he put out a smokescreen of abstract ideas that at least went in support of Mr. Plessy.

So, the majority of the Supremes in <u>Plessy</u> were a bunch of cowards and hacks who when this country was involved in the Civil War to decide its fate, instead of getting involved, they either paid others to do it for them, stuck to their main life's work of paper-pushing, or fought for the confederacy. Based on this reality, Mr. Plessy was doomed from day one. The majority could have gone either way, but based on their personal morality, they decided not to risk another Southern insurrection and ruled against the facts, law, and logic. Did they make the right ethical decision? It is easy for pompous law professors to now spit out political correctness and say 125 years later that <u>Plessy</u> was wrongly decided, but was it ethically decided at the time? The Committee was not willing to risk economic and personal risk to its members, why should the judges to whom it wanted to pass the buck and decision to risk insurrection do it for them — especially when the Committee was not willing to take any personal risks itself? (Apparently, however, in the finest traditions of law firm <u>pro bono</u> work, it was willing to risk the individual client Mr. Plessy getting a criminal record for its ideals.)

Would it really have been the right moral and ethical decision for six white men in judicial robes to take the risk of another violent insurrection in American society in order to force white and blacks to treat each other equally? Did ethics and morality really allow for no other options other than a wide reaching abstract decision that separate but equal is legal under the Constitution? These are the questions and issues of ethics and morality that should have been upfront and discussed by all, including the judges when they made the ethical decision to enforce the Act. Such difficult questions should not be hidden behind a smokescreen of common law that pretends to be objective.

In Plessy, it was a mistake for the Committee to believe that the law would help it at the risk of further weakening an already shaky social order for those in power. Members of the Committee were cowards for not challenging the law by the only way possible for workers to challenge it: by acting outside the law. The irrational Separate Car Act should have been challenged by equally irrational — but just — economic, civil, and outright illegal acts (ones that the Committee could have gotten away with at the time due to the technologically simpler nature of law enforcement) in order to show the law that it would face even greater disorder and weakening of the powers if it did not do something to treat blacks and whites equally.

B. Modern Common Law Decisions: Citizens United v. Federal Election Commission, 558 U.S. 310 (2010); Goodridge v. Department of Public Health, 440 Mass. 309 (Mass. 2003)

The four axioms for reading and interpreting case law apply to all case law, regardless of whether the judges writing it were "liberal" or "conservative", "activist" or "restrained". It applies to all levels of judicial decisions from the simplest traffic hearing to all decisions issued by the Supremes. They all hide the moral and ethical nature of their decisions and that the ethics is always to serve and maintain ruling class ideology. If at any time there occurs any "ethics" requiring a case decision against the ruling class, it would only be a momentary one to counter an unexpected threat to its power; eventually, despite initial practical success, this moment of rebellion against the Party will come around to bite the prols and serve only to further cement the power of the Party.

For a modern application of the four axioms, I am will be applying the axioms to a sample case of a so-called "conservative" decision and of a so called "liberal" decision to show what has changed since Plessy.

It is impossible for a non-lawyer and even for lawyers — though they would not admit it — to read a copy of Citizens United v. Federal Election Commission, 558 U.S. 310 (2010), all of its dozens of pages, depending on what copy you read,

35

and to make any sense of it. What an intellectually dishonest, farcical piece of writing! Unlike <u>Plessy</u> that a reasonably intelligent reader could read, no one — not even a lawyer — can read <u>Citizens</u> and make sense of it despite its simple but far reaching purpose. Its meaning can only be determined pragmatically, that is from the Defendant FEC's actions based on their interpretation of it: this case declared unconstitutional as a violation of 1st Amendment free speech the FEC's ban on corporate and other abstract legal entities' spending on election speech, and, as a general ethical goal, it continued the Supremes' series of decisions making individual persons and abstract legal entities such as corporations equal under the Constitution. According to the Supremes, spending is speech and is protected by the Constitution — even if the speaker is a corporation.

The Supremes could have just as easily gone the other way to say that abstract entities are not persons for the purposes of 1st Amendment speech, especially given that they are not in reality persons but simply legal fictions, but they did not. Nothing in the Constitution, human history, any ontology or metaphysics of life, ethics, or the statutory creation of the legal fiction of a corporation requires that it be equated with human life. Corporations are the creation of mercantilism. In a modern world of insurance indemnification for almost all risks, whether capitalism needs corporations or corporate forms to prosper as a good in society instead of as an evil is a big question that of course the Supremes never asked. Most likely they are not even educated enough in such questions to ask them. <u>Citizens</u> came out the way it did not because of anything written in the Constitution or anywhere, but simply because the Supremes are so in awe of abstract legal fictions and the power they wield, more than any individual person except for the very rich and powerful, of whom they are also in awe. They thus believe that American society and every individual in it must respect such legal fictions as corporations as they would any individual. So, why didn't they just say so?

Instead, what the Supremes and the majesty of the law did was to engage in mental masturbation equivalent to a scientist observing that one apple added to another apple in a basket makes the equivalent of two apples, but instead of expressing such as $1 + 1 = 2$, they write $(8 - 3 - 11) + (15 - 4 + 20 - 30 + 6) + (9 - 15 + 7) = (4 + 4 + 21 - 27)$. Ockham's Razor is not taught in law schools and does not apply to the common law, though it should, as it does in all successful vocations, much of art, and all of the sciences. The Supremes engaged in this mental masturbation, either knowingly and intentionally or ignorantly through their law school indoctrination, to create a smokescreen of an objective common law basis for their moral and ethical decision of equating or making equal before the law abstract legal entities and real individual persons despite purely theoretical options to do otherwise. Making abstract legal entities and real people equal before the law will eventually only serve the powers-that-be and make real people even more powerless. In a matter of a few decades, the Supremes wiped out a couple of millennia of work by Christians trying to make the individual life an end in itself. Man in this new America is most certainly no more the measure of all things. His created abstract legal entities such as corporations are the new measures of all things — real and unreal.

Who are these nine judges who in what is supposed to be a democracy, or at least a republic, had the power and did make this ethical decision for all Americans? The issue was not one of commerce. Before and after Citizens, the legal status of corporations remained the same in the law. What changed was the forced evolution of these legal fictions into "persons" for 1st Amendment protection — a purely political issue. True, corporations and others wanted such evolution so that they could affect the political system to make more money but that is the goal of all politics. Making corporations and other abstract entities equal to "persons" in this attempt to make money is a radical ethical and political change not a commercial one. America has States; if judges did not want to let corporations and individuals work out chaotically among themselves in a social fabric of multiple interventions how they will deal with each other, they could have let the States decide each separately, passed on the decision to the legislature, or decided only the individual parties before them just as Plessy could have let Mr. Plessy on the train as a white person since he passed as white and avoid giving him a criminal record. No, they issued an abstract legal decision to govern the future of all Americans and American culture based on their own morality, without even a discussion of their morality and ethics and ignorant of what the future may hold.

Of the thousands of cases that are filed before them for "*certiorari*" or discretionary review, the modern nobility that makes up the Supremes bows down and takes up less than 1% of them and this had to be one? Who are these King Solomons that they believe God or gods have anointed them with such power?

No one anointed them with such power; they simply took it when offered to them by the powers because they knew they could get away with taking it — as most humans would take on more power if available. This is what law school, the legal culture, and the powers teach them to do. The legal culture takes ambitious individuals who are too cowardly to work in the real world and achieve power by hard physical or mental work and makes them judges. They carry with them the implicit, perhaps unconscious, understanding that in exchange for such an easy life of exercising power they will do whatever is necessary to maintain the status quo of the powers — regardless of whether they must alter the meanings of legal fictions such as corporations to stick it to workers or of social norms such as marriage to keep the workers in disorder and in fear of losing whatever they have and thus less likely to organize and challenge the powers. Sycophants who become judges are all in the same union.

Judges Anthony J. Kennedy, John Roberts, Antonin Gregory Scalia, and Samuel Anthony Alito, Jr. are the usual lifelong power seekers who never thought of anything but their careers and took no risk or position that would risk their ambition to be among the powers and not the powerless at any cost. As someone who spent 12 years in Catholic grammar school and high school, I see them as the big-fish spoiled sons from politically connected, rich, or prosperous Catholic families. They would come to school to control and segregate themselves from any first generation immigrant riffraf from any working class families. They may believe that Christ died for their sins and that God loves them and wants them to rule the earth, but it is doubtful that they ever believed they had any sin to be forgiven or the meek shall inherit the earth. Power is what they always had and always want to have. Scalia was probably the worse lowlife among these sycophants given that one of his hobbies was to shoot caged flightless birds with a shotgun alongside the politicians whom he was supposed to be impartially judging. Shooting the defenseless is a great hobby for a judge.

Judge John Paul Stevens is from a rich, upper-class Chicago family with lawyers all over his family. The powers are and always were his friends.

Judge Ruth Joan Bader Ginsburg truly worked her way up from humble beginnings to be a power in the Outer and Inner Party with the help of her family, friends, and teachers. She did this completely through the legal system, the Outer Party: law school, law clerk, law professor, judge, married to a prominent lawyer, with a child becoming a lawyer. Judge Stephen Breyer worked his way up from non-humble beginnings, his father was a lawyer and his brother also a federal judge, in the same way to become a power in the Inner Party. The law appears to be their religion and it would appear rightly so since it has served them well and given their lives meaning, money, and power.

Judge Clarence Thomas I always find to be a sad case. This is an intelligent, hardworking, and experienced man, but because he is a working class man from a background of poverty the powers do not take him seriously and never have. He rightly has a libertarian view on life because he realizes that if you rely on the powers to help you, even if they appear well-intentioned on the surface, they will always stick it to you and try to beat you back to the ground eventually as they do with all poor in the end. Unfortunately, he is no Willie Brown and was not able to succeed on his own but succeeded in government service to the Outer Party through the powers' constant need to have a black friend around to give political credibility to whatever they are doing. Now that he is in a position of power, he appears too beaten by life to stick it to them and thus will remain a complacent and non-threatening member of the Outer Party excluded from Inner Party life.

Sonia Maria Sotomayor is not a sad case in any way. According to her, she wanted to become a judge since she was in elementary school — that is scary in so many ways. In elementary school and one's goal is to get a lifetime job passing judgment on other people's lives? She must have had quite an ego; good for her given her working class background. She succeeded by determination, hard work, intelligence, and, as always for those who make it out of the working class without having their spirit beaten such as was done to Thomas, a lot of help from an extended family, friends, and much luck. Thanks to the law, she went from being an average paid government bureaucrat to being a millionaire once she received the star status of being a Supreme. Again, as with the others, the law appears to be her religion and rightly so. She wanted a lifelong appointment as a judge to judge other people and control their lives and she got it plus money and power. Whether she will remain an Outer Party gofer or be allowed into the Inner Party is not decided as yet, but no doubt she is ambitious for both.

In summary, the Supremes are made up of flawed humans; given the power that they yield arbitrarily and without accountability, they are much more flawed and much less educated than they should be. So, who gave Sotomayor or any of these Supremes not only the right to make societal changing ethical decisions for all Americans but to do so for life without any accountability for their decisions and without any sophisticated education in ethics or morality? Does the supposed social contract Americans have with the federal government really allow nine people who are appointed for life and are immune from any accountability for their actions make the radical, substantive, moral and social decision of Citizens United? If so, how is this republic not an Athenian Tyranny of the Nine? For workers, there appears to be no substantive or pragmatic difference: in a Technological Society in which workers are becoming essentially just data in an algorithm, the Supremes have decided to formally make workers equal before the law to non-human legal fictions.

In addition to avoiding Ockham's Razor and even the simplicity of Plessy, the Supremes in Citizens United unlike those in Plessy need not worry about any social insurrection or disorder from any decision they make. The Second Amendment is an opiate symbol for the working class with even less pragmatic value then religion. It is, for all practical purposes, impossible for Americans to rebel, civilly or criminally, against a "rule of law" that unjustly makes them economic slaves to the Party and its abstract legal entities. Americans live too much in fear of losing whatever economic or other freedom they have to do any rebelling. If they did anything to act on their thoughts, it would soon gain the attention of either the technology or personnel of the modern, well-paid, well armed, and obeying police forces who will soon put a stop to it using the vast arsenal of available law that increases every year by thousands. Unless the Supremes or any other power in the Party makes the mistake of not paying their law enforcement mercenaries, they have no fear of there ever being any rebellion against any decision they issue.

Goodridge v. Department of Public Health, 440 Mass. 309 (Mass. 2003) shows the ethics and personal morality foundation that is the true factual and reasoning basis for the common law smokescreen, but it also shows how the common law spreads its power to cover all workers: simply by creating fads among judges.

Goodwin makes no sense by any stretch of reason but only based on the changing morals and thus the ethics of ruling class ideology that readily, now at least for the moment, accepts homosexual relations as acceptable. The decision majority consists of four judges; Margaret Marshall wrote the majority opinion in which Judges Roderick L. Ireland, Judith A. Cowin, and John M. Greaney joined. These judges were well known at then and now as the most incompetent judges at the appellate level if not in the court system. Judges Ireland, Cowin, and Greaney were hacks who survived in the law through career government work and succeeded only by their government political connections. Judge Marshall was born in South Africa to an affluent and politically connected family who despite claiming to be against apartheid, instead of staying to fight it, conveniently left when it was clear that her affluence and power will be diminished by the end of apartheid and she went to greener pastures in America. Once here, she proceeded to represent the rich and powerful, including the richest fake nonprofit in Massachusetts: Harvard University, a $40 billion hedge fund that happens to teach classes. She and the others in the majority were well known for their inability to understand any difficult, convoluted, or subtle legal issues, but she excelled at one skill: politics. While living in Cambridge with her rich businessman husband, she was a neighbor of Massachusetts Governor Weld, made sure that she invited him to her parties, and thus smiled her way onto the Supreme Judicial Court, where she made political correctness the new standard of judicial review — unless a legal issue really endangered the power of her rich and powerful friends in Cambridge in which case she always sided with them.

In the smokescreen that is <u>Goodwin</u>, as with <u>Citizens</u>, its conclusion comes down to one moral and ethical issue decided behind the screen by the majority acting as ethicists at best but more likely just as politicians, since it is doubtful that any of them have the education or ability to think as ethicists. As with <u>Citizens</u>, it changed nothing commercially or even physically. <u>Goodwin</u> did not stop any physical attack upon gays; it did not stop any police incursion into their private homes; it did not stop prosecution of private homosexual acts; it did nothing to give protection to gays that did not already exist either in case or statutory law; it made no change to criminal laws protecting or punishing gays or anyone — such as putting millions in jail annually for victimless crimes such as drugs, prostitution, or gambling. Before <u>Goodwin</u>, in America and in the English language throughout history, a perfect example of an analytic logical truth would be "all married couples have a male and female" in the same way the statement "all bachelors are unmarried" would be an example of such. After <u>Goodwin</u> such was neither a logical truth nor even a synthetic one. Granted, there is no such thing in history as a "traditional marriage", but there was such a thing in the Western Civilization of the Christian Era that made us and that became America and whose concepts of Divine and Natural Law are the foundation credibility for all law in Western Civilization: a man and a woman was traditional marriage. <u>Goodwin</u> by a Tyranny of Four redefined marriage without even discussion of any of this religious or even ethical tradition — probably because they were both ignorant of it and lacking in the ability to deal with ethical and moral critical thinking.

How did the ethical decision made by <u>Goodwin</u> spread? Essentially the same way that teenage fashion spreads. Other judges saw <u>Goodwin</u> and how well the majority was treated by the fashionable and said, "oh yeah, I want to wear that too". In a matter of a few years, instead of decades as with the conservative tyrants of <u>Citizens United</u>, many States' common law — but not all — accepted this fad until finally a Tyranny of Five on the United States Supremes decided to wear this fashion and thus negated a couple of millennia of Western morals and ethics and even its language to give marriage a new definition nationally without exception in the United States.

As with <u>Citizens</u>, they need not fear any kind of armed rebellion or even civil rebellion to such conversion of their personal morals into law. If the Christians of this country did not revolt after <u>Roe v. Wade</u> legalized what they considered and consider this day to be murder, they certainly would not do it for the concept of marriage that is a dying tradition in the United States anyway.

So what, the defenders of <u>Goodwin</u> and its progeny respond! This is a <u>Plessy</u> in which the judges need not fear an insurrection if they "protected" the minority

— in this case the minority being gay couples that only the majesty of the law can protect since they are and always will be a minority. This they argue is a Brave New World requiring that we forget the past in order to create the future, and if someone does not agree with this new morality and ethics, the law must force them into accepting this idyllic future in which all will be happy because that is our destiny under the majestic rule of law. They may be right. Thanks to technological biological technique, it may only be a matter of time before society is made up of unisex humans. So, is this the idyllic future that the four unelected politicians who were the Goodwin majority and their groupies through the common law saw in the crystal ball or it this the future they want? Or, is it just that they were so intellectually dullard and lacking in imagination that it never occurred to them that maybe individual American workers' through community interaction should be allowed to consider and make the decision of changing the analytical concept of marriage instead of just their Cambridge cocktail party circle of friends?

Any practical truths about why common law decisions such as Goodwin (and Citizens) issue does not really matter. This argument that the Supremes are protecting a defenseless "minority" is nonsense given both the history of the law, human nature, and the present reality of the law. While the majesty of the law is guaranteeing gays this newly defined concept of marriage, no one seems to notice that every court in the country in unison has 1) engaged in a mass incarceration of our population never before seen in history or in the world except perhaps for the Stalinist or Maoist Purges; 2) assisted and been keystone to a transfer of wealth and thus power to a small elite not seen since Ancient Egypt; and 3) pretty much destroyed of the all powers that the working class fought and died to gain during the last century putting economic slavery in its strongest position in American history. This new right is just another means for the Highs, for whom sex has become just another individual pleasure involving no social conscience other than a "right to choose" that is limited to the mother, to keep the prols and everyone else in their place with broken families and single parent households with children living in poverty arguing about issues that will do nothing to improve their lives.

Further, continuing in this ethical and moral inquiry, one could argue that the analogy to Plessy fails because even if the majority had ruled for Mr. Plessy, it would not have redefined nor given him any right that was not already there; such a decision only would have barred enforcement of a law directed specifically against Plessy, in so far as he identified as a black man.

But such ethical and moral inquiry and argument is a waste. Goodwin is an ethical decision based on personal morals, but it does not and will not admit to being a purely ethical and moral inquiry and decision; instead it hides behind

42

"law". One cannot argue against another's personal morals, they are what they are and only that individual or life will change them. What is important to understand is that through the smokescreen of the common law, the personal morals of the Four Tyrants became the ethics of an entire nation simply by their writing it down while wearing judicial robes. Despite irrational protests denying it, there is no rational difference between allowing gay marriage and allowing polygamy or any other type of marriage involving consensual adults (nor is there any ethical or moral basis to enforce any of the hundreds if not thousands of "victimless" crimes that are laws if personal happiness is the deciding basis for such law). The only bar to any further new legal definitions of marriage is the personal morality of whatever judges will decide the issue and how well paid — and thus loyal — are the police who will enforce it by violence if necessary.

The working class might be more accepting of the concept of having elite enlightened guardian angels with a monopoly of violence and complete lifetime immunity for their acts and no accountability for the consequences being tasked with protecting them — as savage, plebeian, workers — from supposedly evil prejudices, if such a concept had ever worked before in history instead of having the exact opposite effect. In fact, though I have spent my life reading history, I cannot think of any time in history when such a concept of an enlightened elite has worked. The examples of it not working would take weeks and thousands of pages to itemize.

Appellate judges watch from on high the legal battle fought below, and when the dust and smoke of the battle clears they come down out of the hills and shoot the wounded.

Many known and unknown trial lawyers.

VII. EMBRACING THE FAITH AND THE OUTER PARTY

Embracing faith in the law as one's religion and becoming one of its priests as a lawyer or its bishop as a judge involve fairly simple steps — they do not actually require an intense personal leap of faith or special God-given grace as most theologians say is required for Christian faith. Though the average practicing attorney as an individual human being is no better nor worse than the average person trying to survive in life and often is worse off if they have any sense of justice while they practice law, knowing or ignorant delusion of the nature and history of the law and ignorance of the above axioms is a requirement for those who want to be among members of the Outer Party. All members of the Inner Party know the above axioms, but as with any fight club, the number one rule is one must not talk about the fight club. The number one rule for the Party is that its members do not discuss such axioms. The power of the law is based on a fraud and delusion. Therefore, if a practicing attorney wants to be a lifelong member in the Outer Party either as an attorney or a judge, the more shallow and lacking in any *gravitas, pietas, dignitas, and virtus* or even Christian virtues one is, the easier it is both to get the faith and to be initiated as a priest and then to advance as a bishop into the Outer Party that is the law and then into the Inner Party. The unfortunate truth is that usually the better one's reputation as a "professional" lawyer or judge, the more dishonest, culling, and cold-bloodedly unjust such individual will be.

A.   The Client

Though all working class clients and the majority of clients usually do not have the faith, there are some clients that do and who often are members of both the Inner and Outer Party: upper echelon government officials and those who can afford either directly or indirectly to hire these officials for the law's protection.

Explicitly for the entire American criminal law system and implicitly for the American civil law system, the ultimate client for all attorneys and judges is the government. Whenever one hears government prosecutors, politicians, or judges pontificate regarding their concern for victims, that is bullshit. The government controls criminal prosecutions and decides what, when, and how they will be investigated and prosecuted. The choice will always be the one best for the government and not for anyone called a "victim." To avoid private feuds is the point of the criminal law. If such social order must be enforced by social violence, so be it. In fact, the government is by definition the entity in society that has a monopoly on enforcing its orders by violence.

If any self-respecting wealthy suburb had anywhere near an equivalent amount of unsolved murders as we have for the working poor in this country, even a fraction of it, as demonstrated by the recent Boston Marathon and 9/11 bombings but also going back to the multiple Sedition Acts of our American history, no one would give a fuck about the Constitution and there would be an all-out police state put into existence in order to solve unsolved crimes. (In some areas such as New Orleans, in some years, less than 10% of murders involving poor people are solved). In a situation where rich and powerful people felt in any way physically threatened in this country, we would have thousands of police with millions of dollars of equipment, earning millions of dollars in overtime, forcibly closing and searching every neighborhood in any way related and anywhere near the suburb until the perpetrators were caught. The honest truth is that we accept unsolved murders of the poor, both black and white, as the price to be paid for the constitutional protections about which suburban soccer moms and the American intelligentsia (black and white) are most concerned and most in "fear" of losing and for which he and they are willing to pay with the poor's lives — but not theirs of course. Though there was a time when the powers were expected to fight and die for society, thanks to technology, those days are gone. The powers can now sit in comfort and have machines do their killing for them, except for when they have others do their killing for them. The only times they need to get their hands dirty in anyway is when they sit in judgment through the law on those who lose and did the killings for the powers-that-be as "war criminals" — only on the losers, if they win, such is not a concern.

The same is true of the so-called civil justice system that has for all practical purposes gone the way of polo as being now solely a hobby for the rich. Just 25 or 30 years the civil case list for a typical court was much longer than the criminal case list and civil cases would routinely go to trial. Average people were having disputes heard and resolved. However, eventually the large firms in this country realized what a gold mine the billable hour method of billing is thanks to the fake "adversarial" nature of civil litigation. It is adversarial if you can afford the money it takes to make it adversarial. If you can only afford a smart, competent, trial

45

attorney to try with intensity to stick it to the rich and powerful, you and the attorney are being uncivil and combative and will need to be and will be eliminated eventually as uncivil "adversaries". The judges, most of whom these days have no trial experience themselves as attorneys, and if they do, it was as prosecutors in criminal cases, have also realized how cool and empowering it feels to have law large firms generate and file pages of nonsense before them to give their arbitrary rulings a semblance of credibility by hiding the forest in all the trees. Thus, now and for the foreseeable future, the average person cannot afford to hire a lawyer for a truly adversarial litigation or trial proceeding — unless one is crazy and willing to risk financial ruin to do it. What "adversarial" means for practical purposes is not the rare ability to see through convoluted facts and issues to the substance of a manner and present that substance to a judge in all of its logical and factual facets but to generate as much paper as possible on as many nonessential facts and issues so as to generate as many billable hours for as many lawyers as possible.

An experienced trial attorney will tell you — one with at least 25 jury trials taken to verdict — sympathy and empathy with the parties are the key factors that decide trials before juries and by judges. As with the common law, the smokescreen that trial verdicts are based on objective decisions is simply a further way to conceal the ethical and moral basis for all judicial judgments: the law is a system of ethics, not a system of "law". If there ever was a system of law independent of the ethics and morals of those passing judgment, it has not survived into our modern society.

Most clients who suffer the misfortune of getting involved in the American legal system do not care about the law or justice. Justice for them is getting what they want. As lawyers joke among themselves: "How many clients does it take to change a lightbulb? One, they hold the bulb and expect the world to revolve around them." For working class people, this is how it should be. The law does not care and will not take care about you; if you do not watch out for yourself, no one will, often not even your lawyer. The few lawyers who try to work and win difficult cases for working class clients will eventually suffer financial and personal ruin, because the last thing either the criminal or the civil injustice system wants is an intelligent, honest, hardworking lawyer working for the prols without their approval and limitations.

B.   Law School

It is at law school that creation of the oligarchy that is legal culture begins. At present, law school operates as and is essentially a bad vocational school pretending to be an academic institution. Law school requires little if any intellectual rigor and discipline, yet because a few of its members and graduates go on to hold great power in society over the lives and livelihood of many, some — Harvard Law, Yale, and such similar oligarchies — hold much prestige. Law professors achieve "scholar" status by writing law review articles about case law in which there is no empirical or even analytic study of the case law but only a statement of personal opinion that no one reads except for other professors. Why any law professor's opinion of case law should be given any more value than any other person's opinion of case law is never stated. It is just assumed that their opinion is worth something because they are professors. It is typical of the hypocritical nature of the law that it claims to protect equality for all through a completely unequal, oligarchical, prestige based educational system with no desire or basis to conceptualize a meritocracy for teaching, scholarship, or anything dealing with law school.

Exactly what is this law school that ends with the student receiving a *juris doctore*, a doctorate of law, degree that is the first step of initialization into the Outer Party? Such a degree was actually one of the first to be granted in the earliest development of the university concept in the Middle Ages at the University of Bologna in the 13th Century. However, at that time, the emphasis was law as a philosophy and theology. It was the study of ethics and morals operating in the context and means of secular government — there was no study of "case" law but cannon law. The basic premise of modern American law school education is founded upon a 19th Century view begun in Germany and then continued at Harvard University. It believes the law is a science that can be studied separately from other disciplines, with the law library as the laboratory, and the case law within the library providing the basic principles or doctrines from which all law present and future can be logically deducted. Thus, from its first moment and premise for being, the modern American law school is a fraud.

Continuing the concept of law as a science to the practical aspect that theory must be tested against results is completely absent from any law school curriculum or "scholarship" because such would require real work from Outer Party law professors that may result in revealing the true axioms for interpreting the common law and thus endanger their status as powers in the law. This is even true of the "law and economics" law school crowd who pretend to want to base law on economic principles yet there is no study of economic theory in law school nor in the case law written by such "law and economics" judges who continue the fraud that their decisions are based on prior case law. There is no concept or scholarly admission or study of the basic economic principles of a capitalist society consisting of the true golden rule: he who has the gold makes the rules. Though lawyers and especially future judges want to make history, there is no history studied in law school. They want to make ethical decisions for society, but study no ethical theories or critiques or critical thinking in law school. They want to make economic and scientific decisions, yet study neither economics nor any theory of what science is. Above all, the future judges want to be politicians without the hassle of studying and getting involved in politics.

This fraud continues throughout law school. The first year is spent on learning the basics of law usually consisting of courses in contract, criminal law, torts, and property law. Such is usually taught by professors who have never actually practiced for any significant period in any of these areas, who instead teach these subjects by having the students study case law on these subjects. The whole of these basics could be taught in a six-week course plus six weeks to learn the intricacies of navigating through the library of available materials on case law and statutory law plus maybe three to six months at most of mock trial and moot court experience. Thus, for any college graduate with even average writing and reading skills, law school could be done in six months followed by graduation and then sent out to practice as apprentice attorneys.

So, what the heck goes on for the next more than two years to spend three years on what should be a 12 week vocational school? Most of the above average or honest and intelligent law students that I have met who want to actually practice and do practice upon graduation, unless they have political ambitions of being a judge or of an life of ease as a law professor, usually stop going to class at the end of the first year and just show up for finals for the next two years. Actually attending classes for the entire three years of law school, to any college graduate with even a minimal amount of honesty, intelligence, and critical thinking ability is mind-numbing to the point of contemplating suicide. The last two years are for those who want to be judges, politicians, or law professors. By actually taking those two years seriously and engaging in the mental masturbation that is reading and pretending to analyze case law, they prove they have the faith and complete self-centered ambition for power combined with fear of real-world law practice necessary to be a judge or law professor.

Law professors are relatively harmless since no one pays any attention to them outside of law school, not even the judges who kissed their behinds while in law school in order to get good grades, but they serve as an example of how hypocritical law schools are. Just two examples demonstrate the joke that law school and law professors are.

In a recent editorial article, former federal judge Nancy Gertner, now a law professor at Harvard Law School, complained about how draconian federal sentencing requirements are and how she hated to sentence so many people to harsh sentences. No one has called her on such hypocrisy. She was a politically connected attorney who marketed herself well to the point of getting a federal judgeship in which she had life tenure and essentially no accountability to anyone. While on the bench, trial attorneys knew her as the inventor of federal court "Gertner Time", in by 10AM out by 4PM and little work done in-between for the few months she was in session. The whole point of such life tenure and lack of accountability supposedly was so that she can do justice and avoid "draconian" decisions and sentences. She had almost unlimited power to twist and turn the "law" to reach whatever decision she wanted or at least to go on the record and publicize what was going on. She did nothing when she had the unchecked power to do it, waited until she was retired with a secure, well paying nonsense job as a professor, and then writes about "draconian" sentencing in an editorial piece that no one with power will read or do anything about? Other than getting her name in the paper (something she no doubts misses) and further strengthening her political correctness cred among her groupies, what was the point? There was no other point nor any other benefits.

Other Harvard Law School professors as part of some nonsense symposium recently complained, based on their one-year experience as big firm lawyers that is usually mandatory after their one or two-year experience as law clerks before becoming law professors, of "frivolous" intellectual property litigation. The complaint was that as associates, their big firm spent millions on defending "frivolous" litigation brought by evil plaintiffs but then had to settle it to avoid the expense of a trial. As any competent trial attorney will tell you, there is nothing easier than defending a "frivolous" case. One essentially files an answer and then waits for a trial notice. At this point, usually one of two things will happen, either the judge will find a way to get rid of the case or the plaintiff will go away voluntarily to avoid the expense of a trial on a contingent fee basis. This usually means they are not paid for their work. The only attorneys that would spend "millions" on defending a frivolous case are big firms who do so to generate paper and billable hours on a "frivolous" defense.

Law schools market themselves as valuing "diversity", however any open mind capable of critical thought would find law school intellectually closed and depressing except for those with an egotistical need for power without risk. Law school intellectually goes from one form of mental masturbation legal culture fad to another usually without even noticing the switch. Students take the common courses during the first year in which they avoid any politically incorrect disputes or argument. The next two years of courses are based on the students' political preferences, with conservatives taking courses such as corporations, taxation, trusts, and clinical courses pursuing criminal prosecution, while liberal students take the opposite politically correct courses to support their beliefs — all the while avoiding any diverse opinions or argument that would contradict what they came to law school believing. Students want to make history but study no history. The ambitious want to go on to force ethical and moral judgment upon society but do not study either ethical or moral theory and avoid any critical thinking in either. There is diversity of sex and race perhaps but no diversity of ideas or thinking. As with almost all of undergraduate and post-graduate education, there is almost no diversity of economic class and no mingling among whatever economic diversity may exist.

The shallowness of law school thought is exemplified by the recent dispute and decision by Harvard Law School, a supposed center of critical legal thinking, to eliminate its code of arms or seal that was as follows:

Anyone with a basic knowledge of history will first notice that this seal uses the Roman expression of "veritas" meaning truth as its motto — as does the Harvard University seal. Until the advent of Muslim empires, the Roman Empire's legal system was the largest in the Western World to recognize slavery as an acceptable, legally enforced social class and legal status that lasted among the poor Slavs of Europe well into the 18th Century (from which derived our word "slave"). Even for those familiar with history, it is the rare person who knows that the three haystack emblems (haystacks symbolize knowledge that grows anew each year in the same way that grain grows anew each year) on the seal are taken from the coat of arms of Isaac Royall Jr., a slaveholder who endowed the first professorship of law at Harvard more than 200 years ago. After a great amount of committee meetings and memoranda, did the great legal minds at Harvard use this as an opportunity to read and study history to learn how much of its greatness — for all practical purposes, all of it — derives from the hard work and suffering of millions of workers both slave and serfs of the past whose masters decided to donate part of their riches from that hard work and suffering to the improvement of society through education? Did they use this as an opportunity to study philosophies of history to think critically about the dialectic of history? Did they use it as an opportunity at least to examine their own lives to see what hypocrisy they may be living either as supposed professors or attorneys? Such as for example, the fact that they run Harvard and the legal profession through a plantation governing system in which the top consists of individuals of supposedly superior ethics known as "overseers"? Did the decide to keep eliminate the professorship funded by that blood money and donate that present value of it to the poor? Did they decide to keep the logo in specific memory and honor of those slaves? None of this. The shallow conclusion, predetermined to occur from the moment the politically correct ruling O'Briens of Harvard Law raised the issue, was to concentrate on the seal element stacks of wheat and remove them thus putting form over substance that exemplifies the entire nature of law school.

C. Judges

So, after completing the mind-numbing experience that is law school by actually attending and taking it seriously for an entire three years, either because one is so ambitious for the power to pass judgements on the lives of others or one is too clueless to read and understand the history of law, how does one become a judge, a bishop in the Outer Party? It has nothing to do with experience, intelligence, or honesty — in fact, all of these virtues are more a hindrance than aid. A person has to be fairly egotistical to be a judge as a career and not as a part-time calling based on experience, empathy, and intelligence. Basically, for the vast majority of the work, a trial judge sits in judgment of other peoples' lives, cold-bloodedly views their problems, and then makes their lives worse in some way so as to maintain whatever social order exists — be it the order of a North Korean dictatorship, a Russian oligarchy, or an American oligarchy. The order is always maintained by the sacrifice of the individual — unless the judge is sympathetic to the individual — with all decisions usually required to be universal and not accepting of diversity or individual personality. There is no curing of disease, no invention, no epiphany, no theorem proven, no joy of pure analytical thought, no joy of experiment, no critical thinking to a solution, no scientific method, no glory of winning, and no agony of defeat — any type of honest emotion and good faith belief in a principle or good is to be avoided (other than "law and order" that actually means just order). The only joy is in the power of playing god — however, the judge cannot admit to such playing but must hide behind the smokescreen of common law, pretending that there is something more there than just arbitrary decisions of what personal ethics and morals to enforce and which not to enforce.

Appellate judges' work is even more soulless. They sit behind the battle lines a safe distance from the smoke of battle; wait for the battle to rage and end through exhaustion of the combatants and the smoke to clear; and then calmly come forward to view the devastation and shoot the wounded. For this safe work that involves almost no risk to them, they require as do the trial judges who have a little more risk, life tenure with no accountability for their work product. That appellate judges can do such soulless work for a life time demonstrates how power hungry they are and their cowardice. These facts speak for themselves as to the delusion that the law is in any way a system of justice.

The universal rule for being a judge is to hide and deny the validity and soundness of the Four Axioms for interpreting case law. Legal "truth" actually depends on fraud, from the first day of law school to the last day of a 70+ year old judge's issuance of case law.

It is becoming much easier for judges to get away with this fraud because attorneys with enough experience and the courage to confront them are becoming rare. As many as ninety percent of attorneys go through their whole career without appearing in court on behalf of a client. These days, if an attorney has done one or two trials in their career, they are a "trial attorney". You do not even need that many appellate arguments to be an "appellate attorney", just the filing of a brief is enough. The attorney world is full of "litigators" who charge a lot of money to move paper from one side of their desk to the other. Very few attorneys have the necessary experience of at least 10 or more complete jury trials taken to verdict and appellate arguments that would give them the experience and confidence to take on judges for their fraud — even fewer who are willing to do so once they have the experience. For major courts such as the U.S. Supreme Court and almost any administrative court, such as a local bankruptcy court, there is essentially a small club of attorneys that handles a large percentage of the case load and thus have no incentive to challenge the inherent fraud of whatever court in which they regularly appear as it is the source of their income. As I said above, the rest of the legal world feeds off the need to "interpret" the common law generated by judges as the basis for establishing their livelihood and therefore has no reason to challenge it even if they understand the fraud that it perpetuates.

By any measurement of relative success — especially relative to our society's technological progress of the past 100 years — the American legal system and most legal systems are complete failures in achieving their pretended goal: a working system of justice for all individuals in their communities. So much so that in the United States the legal culture has for all practical purposes given up on the concept of "justice" to replace it with an equally abstract concept of "due process" that the law successfully — at least for the moment — markets as being much better than justice. However, its ultimate success depends not solely on marketing but on fear and upon a symbiosis with government's monopoly on violence. The symbiosis consists of the law acting as a secular religion whose ethics justifies the government's monopoly on violence that in turn provides the law with the enforcer it needs to compel compliance with its secular religious ethics.

D.   The Business of Law

If the law was ever a profession, it is no longer. It is a business and a cutthroat one. Most of the big money lawyers dependent on an hourly fee to get rich do so by using an army of wage slave associates and fake non-equity partners to generate that money. Thanks to the billable hour method of billing, for the big firms the key character traits necessary for success are incompetence as a lawyer — that is a complete lack of the intellectual ability clearly to see to the substance of a case — matched with amoral political instincts. Successful contingent fee lawyers spend their time like vultures circling for the most sympathetic cases such as dead babies or "quad" cases or technically strong class actions high in quantity but low in quality. Government lawyers spend their time hoping their government service will eventually get them a well-paid private job as a rainmaker or just let them survive until their pensions kick in. The remainder are just trying to survive like most people in society and are no different than any other business or employees except for having a board of "overseers" to make sure they comply with the arbitrary rules created by the Inner Party and their Outer Party enforcers designed solely not to threaten their business practices.

Progress isn't made by early risers. It's made by lazy men trying to find easier ways to do something.

Robert A. Heinlein

VIII. OPTIONS

There is so much convoluted and inconsistent law that changes on a daily if not hourly basis and that makes no sense either analytically or pragmatically that we essentially live in a lawless society pretending to be governed by the "rule of law". What are the options for a working man or woman to survive and to try to change this new unopposed secular religion of the law? Not much either in practice or in theory — the main goal for now is survival until something comes up as was often the main goal for the majority of workers in all eras. For the few that care, at the end of this essay, I provide a list of simple changes that would create significantly more freedom and reduce the tyranny of arbitrary law, but that I admit have no chance of being implemented in the foreseeable future. My intent in proposing them is to give a general concept or basic elements of a foundation to an opposing culture to the present illusion of law. For now, it is more important to have some method for living that workers can use to survive the tyranny of law by judges until an opposing culture comes to life, or if one never comes to life, as a way of living under its dangling sword.

In terms of changing its power to a more democratic basis, there is nothing that can be done. Historically, the only option against tyrants was open and violent physical rebellion, supported by those in power who were jealous of the tyrant. Even if modern Western citizens are mentally capable of such an option in large enough numbers to be a serious threat, thanks to technology it would essentially be suicide that would only make matters worse. This new modern tyranny of the law is not really just one of the Five or Four or One, it consists of an entire normative social and cultural structure that is greater than the few who at any given time have been chosen to be its preachers and enforcers. The events of "9/11" in the United States exemplify this reality. The tragedy caused by a handful of religious zealots rebelling against secular Western Civilization was the result of government incompetence. Those in power had plenty of notice and opportunity to prevent it. Having failed to do so, no government agent was held responsible for the incompetence. Instead, the government was allowed to get bigger and gather even further power, start two wars, make a further mess of everything, get paid more for this mess, and the law not only allowed all this to occur but contributed to the power gathering of the Party by its own dilution of the only available constitutional means to control it. While doing all of this surrendering of freedom, the law pretended to be a protector of the powerless by assuming that Islam is a religion and not a political system as it was first intended to be when created by Mohammed and that it is and also by re-defining marriage for the benefit of gay couples thus assuring that the working class and religious in the United States — the only viable opponents to government power — would be busy fighting among themselves on these new issues in the same way that they were already fighting over abortion. The Second Amendment as with all law is only an illusion, it is not an option for battle.

A.   "To Punish and Enslave" through the law and wage slavery

The civilian enforcers of the law, the police at all levels of government, are now a professional, well paid, well compensated force made up of individuals that in different eras might have been rebels against the law or criminals before it, but now they have seen the light: life is much easier and better compensated if one acts as a Praetorian Guard for this modern emperor the law. At present, they will enforce any rulings issued by the law, and the Outer Party need not worry about any rebellion to its arbitrary power. As they become more powerful, as with the Pretorian Guard of the Roman Empire, they will have the power to change the nature of the law — however, whether and when they will change it and to what is an unknown.

As written by George Orwell, this modern ruling Party exists independently of any of its members. As he so eloquently pointed out, unlike other tyrannies from individual dictatorships to class dictatorships such as communism and even Islam, it survives the death or destruction of both its Outer Party and Inner Party members:

"Now I will tell you the answer to my question. It is this. The Party seeks power entirely for its own sake. We are not interested in the good of others; we are interested solely in power. Not wealth or luxury or long life or happiness; only power, pure power. What pure power means you will understand presently. We are different from all the oligarchies of the past in that we know what we are doing. All the others, even those who resembled ourselves, were cowards and hypocrites. The German Nazis and the Russian Communists came very close to us in their methods, but they never had the courage to recognize their own motives. They pretended, perhaps they even believed, that they had seized power unwillingly and for a limited time, and that just round the corner there lay a paradise where human beings would be free and equal. We are not like that. We know that no one ever seizes power with the intention of relinquishing it. Power is not a means; it is an end. One does not establish a dictatorship in order to safeguard a revolution; one makes the revolution in order to establish the dictatorship. The object of persecution is persecution. The object of torture is torture. The object of power is power. Now do you begin to understand me?"

...

"We are the priests of power," he said. "God is power. But at present power is only a word so far as you are concerned. It is time for you to gather some idea of what power means. The first thing you must realize is that power is collective. The individual only has power in so far as he ceases to be an individual. You know the Party slogan 'Freedom is Slavery.' Has it ever occurred to you that it is reversible? Slavery is freedom. Alone-free-the human being is always defeated. It must be so, because every human being is doomed to die, which is the greatest of all failures. But if he can make complete, utter submission, if he can escape from his identity, if he can merge himself in the Party so that he is the Party, then he is all-powerful and immortal. The second thing for you to realize is that power is power over human beings. Over the body-but, above all, over the mind. Power over matter external reality, as you would call it-is not important. Already our control over matter is absolute."

...

"How does one man assert his power over another, Winston?"
Winston thought. "By making him suffer," he said.
"Exactly. By making him suffer. Obedience is not enough. Unless he is suffering, how can you be sure that he is obeying your will and not his own?"

To oppose the tyranny of legal culture requires an equally strong opposing culture. At present, there is none. Christianity has let its principles be hijacked by the law without a fight and through its own incompetence. Mormonism seems to be a religion created by lawyers. It might be a long time until an opposing culture is created, if ever. The key lies in creating an opposing culture not in changing the legal culture. It will only change if forced to do so by an opposing culture.

Given the destruction occurring in the modern world of Western religion and all other non-law social support and relationships, my biggest fear is that modern wage slavery will destroy whatever individual strength there is to fight the powers and the Party and thus make our unavoidable future consist of the law's goal of a Brave New World made up of soulless power seekers. (I do not consider Islam a religion, regardless of what it calls itself. A warrior religion is politics and one such as Islam is a Master Morality that will always empower the powers-that-be and rule by judges regardless of its pretensions otherwise.) Though formal slavery under the law has been eliminated from the United States through the sacrifice of many a workingman in the Civil War, the new arising institution of wage slavery in the modern world is supported by the law in the same way it supported chattel slavery though it is too cowardly to admit what it is doing.

Wage slavery is just as bad if not worse than chattel slavery because it destroys humanity's soul and not just the body. Ancient societies were more sophisticated than ourselves in contemplating the morality and ethics of slavery both in chattel or legal form and in the form of wage slavery. Ancient philosophers such as Aristotle, Alcidamas, and Euripides considered and wrote on this issue and even political theorists such as Cicero in the Roman Republic considered it. Alcidamas and Euripides concluded that slavery was ethically and morally wrong. Until the rise of Christianity, these views were in the minority. Most such as Aristotle and Cicero concluded that chattel slavery was ethically and morally better than wage slavery because it maintained social relationships of support and duty between master and slave whereas there was none in wage slavery between the employer and employee: the employer simply had to pay wages for certain work and could discard the worker at any time with no obligation to provide for the welfare and support of that worker. Thus, according to this view, the wage worker lived a life of complete insecurity and lack of social relationship that fostered disorder and chaos instead of civilized society. Every economic analysis comparing the health, lifespan, and social and material wealth of Southern slaves with their wage earning but "legally free" counterparts in Northern factories or on farms has concluded that the slaves as individuals actually had better health, longer life spans, and more economic and social stability including family stability. Modern polemics makes much of the slave families in which some members were separated and sold off to other masters but ignores the much more common event of working class families sending a father, brother, daughter, uncle, and many more relatives out into the world, with the boys as young as ten years old, to earn wages either as voluntary or forced labor or state sponsored conscription for the powers but then never to return nor be heard from again.

Unlike legal chattel slavery, the benefit of wage slavery used to be that it allowed for the worker to build social relationships of power with his fellow workers that could challenge the powers-that-be: fraternal organizations, mass meetings, revolts, unions, benevolent organizations, clubs, and all sorts of social groups in as many versions and names going back to ancient economies such as the Roman plebeians' clashes with the ruling patricians of Rome in 495 and 494 BC that led to the creation of the special tribunes in the Senate to represent the plebeians and to protect them from the power of the consuls. Thanks to the majesty of the law, modern technology, and the fear that dominates the modern world, such building of social relationships of power between individual workers united by ethnicity, work, sex, or misery is no longer possible. Before the modern technological world, such social groups uniting outside of the law for the purpose of improving the lives of workers was possible because the powers did not have the physical, technological means to control it — now it would be social suicide if not individual suicide for any worker attempting it. The only way that a social power can now be created is through politics or the law: but their whole purpose is to prevent the creation of any such opposing power, especially in the form of a united front of workers. It is a Catch-22 situation for which no solution now exists.

B.   There must be No Fear nor Blind Respect — do not pull a Plessy

Since armed rebellion is no longer an option, the only other option is civil disobedience when one thinks one can get away with it. What this disobedience will entail varies on each person's life. Again, as with most eras, most workers simply want to survive and do not care about the nature of the government that controls them — "meet the new boss same as the old boss."

For those that do care, it is most important not to pull a Plessy and expect the law to protect or help you in anything. Any worker who expects and seeks protection from the law is either a fool or a coward. The more law that is created the more power that is given to the Outer Party and thus to the Party and Inner Party. The law should be the last possible option for help because it will only help workers when it is forced to do so — if help is sought, there must be a counterbalance to the use of this option. For now, every new law created should result in the elimination of at least 100 other laws or regulations so that eventually through Ockham's Razor there is reached an understandable equilibrium of law and anarchy. We live in a complicated world of science and technology that will only get more complicated. The Outer Party and its bishop judges have no incentive to simplify it nor to deal with substance instead of form as lawyers are supposed to do and that should be their primary social contribution. From the billable hour system of the big firms that control litigation to the hack judges with no experience who are impressed by how much verbiage they can issue, the law has no concept of Ockham's Razor and the benefit it serves both for a rational understanding of society and for its equitable operation.

For example, there are Americans who believe that abortion is essentially murder. The rational argument can be made that abortion is the last form of legalized slavery wherein an unborn child is reduced to being property of the mother. However, abortion proponents keep going back to the same judges who legalized abortion to try to make it illegal. The process has been and will continue to be a failure. If this is the best with which they can come up to oppose what they believe is murder, then it may be that Divine Law is really not on their side.

The only advantage that a working man or woman has against the tyranny of law by judges is the courage and the strength of will to endure and overcome hardship. Most judges — especially among the federal court life tenure bench — are incredibly lazy and scared of losing their power and of anyone that disrespects their authority. It is incredible as to how many judges I have run across who are trust fund babies by inheritance or by marriage yet still need the security of a federal judicial appointment to feel safe in life. Their goal in life is to become gods. They leave home in the morning, go to a job they can never lose and for which they have no accountability, in which they are surrounded by worshipers who adorn all their wishes as commandants no matter how stupid they are. If anyone dares to disrespect their authority, they send that person to jail.

Once this advantage of courage and will is lost and fear runs a worker's life, the law has won.

As I pointed out earlier, Americans by tradition and culture have been rebels and disrespectful of government and law. This recent marketing of America as a nation run by the rule of law is just that, marketing. It is no more true than the fraud that judges are objective rulers of fact and law. We must accept such disrespect as our own world view again and not fear the consequences. The powers will try to scare you by marketing that without the rule of law we will become an anarchy, a Syria or an Iraq. Bullshit. As Americans we must have more confidence in ourselves and our belief in Christian virtues that existed and that exist independently of the law and that the law has hijacked, distorted, and diluted to give itself credibility.

Democracies and republics have come and gone in history. The Athenian democracy rightly fell because it became a plutocracy, wasting its free citizens' lives on wasteful wars. Those few who were still free to live as they wished and ambitious and intelligent enough to survive the fall of Athens willingly went over to its conquerors, including the Roman Republic that in turn fell into dictatorship because of the same problems. As a result of all the courage of the Republic's people, that mess became the Roman Empire and then the Holy Roman Empire and Christianity instead of sitting in a decrepit pretend republic or democracy that was nothing it pretended to be.

Workers must not fear change or temporary anarchy or even the destruction of a democracy that is such in name only, in the end, no fear is our only weapon.

The only hope, unfortunately, for avoiding a 1984 culture in American culture is the threat of or happening of a similar disaster as fell the Athenian democracy and the Roman Republic. The law has become an independent oligarchy. Our government has no Roman *Tribunus Plebis* to formally represent working class interests, supposedly this occurs naturally through our three branches of government. If such was ever true, it is clearly no longer true given the wealth and income disparity in this country. The legislative branch of government is essentially a training ground and club for future lobbyists who will come back to tell future legislatures how to help the rich and powerful stay rich and powerful. The executive branch is quickly becoming an appointed Roman dictator that will only become more powerful while also becoming more incompetent as time goes on because, for now, only ambitious people with no experience in life seek the presidency because running for political office has become a full time campaigning, soliciting, and bullshit generating job that allows for proficiency and ability in nothing but bullshitting. It is only a matter of time before a modern day Augustus Caesar comes along as a non-appointed dictator to put a stop to the nonsense. We need not fear such an event.

The ancient Greeks and Romans were much more sophisticated than any modern politician or political theorist in understanding the realities of maintaining the virtues of a successful *polis*: wisdom, courage, moderation, and justice. Yet, they failed at maintaining a democracy or republic due to its corruption by the wealth of the upper classes. Christianity was supposed to be the difference and create a Holy Roman Empire that would last — but it also failed in avoiding the same corruption. If our rule-by-judges society with its fraudulent "rule of law" and democratic ideals — violated on a daily basis by the powers — fails to give us a decent livelihood, freedom, and a culture that prospers and seeks to explore and conquer the universe as was intended by the honored living and dead who served and fought to create this country, then let us go on to try something else to achieve these goals. Do not fear such a cultural change as the powers fear it, especially the

60

cowardly tyrants of the Outer Party. To paraphrase another country's rebels: we have nothing to lose but our chains — modern common law chains that destroy the soul and not the body which is worse.

This courage and will must include no fear of technology. As I pointed out earlier, probably the only significant changes that have increased modern legal culture's fact finding accuracy when compared to older traditions is its use of technology such as DNA testing. Otherwise it would be still stumping around in the dark no better than medieval trials by ordeal or Rome's *Basilica Julia*. Modern legal culture's monopoly on violence making physical rebellion impossible is dependent on technology. In a short time, judges may not even need mercenary police to execute their monopoly but will be able to do so through robotic drones ruining workers' lives solely at the judge's will, a wonder weapon that will be a dream come true for judges — they no longer will need have any concern for maintaining their power through reliance on human police. It will complete law as a secular god by giving it direct power to kill as real gods do without human intermediaries. Paraphrasing George Patton, "Wonder weapons? My God, I don't see the wonder in them. Killing without heroics. Nothing is glorified, nothing is reaffirmed. No heroes, no cowards, no troops. No humanity, no emotion, and no soul involved. Only those that are left alive and those that are left ... dead." This will be the Brave New World of the law. It is not and will not be possible to fight this Brave New World solely by Beatitudes. It will take an equally strong and successful technological or scientific counter-culture of rebellion.

C.   Substantive Option: Use and Create Arbitration/Private Options that Admittedly Use Ethics and Morality

Again, the only weapons that we have against the Outer Party are its own laziness and that it should fear us more than we fear them. Out of their laziness, both mentally and physically, and not realizing the opportunity it gave or underestimating the ingenuity of *hoi polloi*, they have created strong and numerous case law preferring and enforcing arbitration of civil cases. Arbitrators have almost unlimited authority, as long as they commit no corruption or fraud, to decide cases with no appellate review — there is no appeal of legal or factual errors by an arbitrator. This grants us an enormous opportunity to create an almost independent legal system for civil cases. For example, there is no reason why Christians could not set up a contract defined arbitration system in which the arbitrators would be ministers, priests, Christian laypersons, or whoever they want who will arbitrate cases based on Christian principles. As long as there is a contractual agreement for such arbitration among the parties, the law should enforce it, and, if it does not all of a sudden because the arbitration alternative becomes too powerful, it will be an obvious showing by the law of an arbitrary act taken to protect its own power and thus may be an incentive to diminish that power. By creating such an independent judicial system, if enough of society is involved, it has the potential of eventually being a competitor to the secular religion that is the law.

There should be as many attempts as possible to set up as many private systems of justice, mediation, arbitration, and consolidation as possible in the hope that at least one will catch on as an alternative culture, a counterbalance to the present monopoly held by American legal culture. Again, one must not fear any temporary disorder that such might cause, it is their fear of such disorder that will allow for progress in the same way that the disorder of the 1950s and 1960s finally led to overthrowing the Jim Crow laws resulting from Plessy. If the Committee in Plessy had taken that route back in the 19th Century instead of weakly and fearfully falling before the law to protect them, they probably could have avoided the 100 years of Jim Crow and the misery and backwardness that it caused for a large part of America.

Such alternative cultures of justice must not repeat the fraud of present legal culture and hide behind claims that its arbitrators, mediators, or whatever it calls its "judges" or "juries" are objective finders of "fact" and "law". It must admit that it is making ethical decisions based on the decision makers' ethics or morality and state outright what that ethics or morality is and how it factors into and causes their fact finding and decisions of their "just" resolution of the case before them.

D. Procedural Options

1. No Appointed Life Tenure

The alleged reason for lifetime political appointments of hacks to judgeships is so that they can act independently and without fear of political repercussions. There is no proof that this works and no one is attempting to prove or disprove it. In my trial experience and in the experience of all trial attorneys that I have met, it does not work. Political appointments are just that, political appointments. The appointee is someone who spent a lifetime avoiding belief and experience in anything that would risk their career. Their only loyalty is to themselves and to the politics that got them there. The idea that such a person would act independently and without fear of political repercussions is nonsense. All available studies show no lack of competence by elected judges compared to appointed judges, but only that they issue less and shorter decisions. If an attorney is so much of a coward that he needs a lifetime appointed government judgeship to act with fairness and impartiality, this attorney has no business being a judge. I and all trial attorneys that I have met have not found appointed judges any more courageous, fair, or impartial than elected judges. To receive a political appointment as a judge, a lawyer must essentially sell his soul to such task and avoid taking — at least publicly — any strong positions or believing passionately on anything. Such appointments go only to those whose qualifications are that they have led sheltered, noncommittal lives, usually as non-trial prosecutors, big firm lawyers generating billable hours, or as government bureaucrats who upon appointment are then magically expected to become emotionally strong and tested human beings capable of making tough but fair choices and decisions — this is absurd. They remain what they were: attorneys whose main goal in life was to use political clout to get the secure job of a judge.

For humans, power corrupts, and absolute power corrupts absolutely. Until the Executive Branch becomes an dictatorship, there is no more absolute power in government right now than a federal judge appointed for life. Right now, most are incompetent to begin with at appointment; this situation gets worse as the power of life tenure is added into the mixture.

Judicial appointments should be limited in tenure. Elected judges as with all elected officials should have term limits. No judge should be in either an appointed or elected judicial position unless they have taken at least 25 trials to verdict and not all be criminal or civil trials. If there are not enough qualified candidates, draft some. The legal system must be set up to allow for attorneys to get such experience.

2. *The Parties should have the Last Word in a Judicial Decision*

Right now, judicial decisions occur after oral arguments before a judge or judges who in many cases has not bothered to learn the case or even read the facts but who then issues a decision. In courts of appeals, such pretend argument sometimes lasts only ten minutes. The judge or judges then issue a decision that forever defines the facts and law of the case even though, as the above axioms state, there is usually no relationship between the facts and law stated on appeal and what actually happened in the trial court or in the world.

Judges must issue their decisions first based on the evidence and filed written argument before them. This decision must then be followed by oral argument if the parties request it.

63

Finally, when a decision is issued, the parties must be allowed to attach to it their final objections or rebuttal pointing out what they consider to be errors. The parties should have the last word on the merits of the case for future generations that may read the decision not the judge who already has the last word on how it is to be decided and on its execution.

There is respect for law, and then there is complicity in lawlessness.

Rebecca MacKinnon

IX.   CONCLUSION

Finally and again, there is so much convoluted and inconsistent law that is created and changes on a daily if not hourly basis and that makes no sense either analytically or pragmatically that we essentially live in a lawless society that only pretends to be governed by the "rule of law". I will leave the last words of this essay to be by George Orwell:

> Now I will tell you the answer to my question. It is this. The Party seeks power entirely for its own sake. We are not interested in the good of others; we are interested solely in power. Not wealth or luxury or long life or happiness; only power, pure power. What pure power means you will understand presently. We are different from all the oligarchies of the past in that we know what we are doing. All the others, even those who resembled ourselves, were cowards and hypocrites. The German Nazis and the Russian Communists came very close to us in their methods, but they never had the courage to recognize their own motives. They pretended, perhaps they even believed, that they had seized power unwillingly and for a limited time, and that just round the corner there lay a paradise where human beings would be free and equal. We are not like that. We know that no one ever seizes power with the intention of relinquishing it. Power is not a means; it is an end. One does not establish a dictatorship in order to safeguard a revolution; one makes the revolution in order to establish the dictatorship.
>
> ...
> ...Do you begin to see, then, what kind of world we are creating? It is the exact opposite of the stupid hedonistic Utopias that the old reformers imagined. A world of fear and treachery and torment, a world of trampling and being trampled upon, a world which will grow not less but more merciless as it refines itself. Progress in our world will be progress toward more pain. The old civilizations claimed that they were founded on love and justice. Ours is founded upon hatred. In our world there will be no emotions except fear, rage, triumph, and self-abasement. Everything else we shall destroy- everything. Already we are breaking down the habits of thought

which have survived from before the Revolution. We have cut the links between child and parent, and between man and man, and between man and woman. No one dares trust a wife or a child or a friend any longer. But in the future there will be no wives and no friends. Children will be taken from their mothers at birth, as one takes eggs from a hen. The sex instinct will be eradicated. Procreation will be an annual formality like the renewal of a ration card. We shall abolish the orgasm. Our neurologists are at work upon it now. There will be no loyalty, except loyalty toward the Party. There will be no love, except the love of Big Brother. There will be no laughter, except the laugh of triumph over a defeated enemy. There will be no art, no literature, no science. When we are omnipotent we shall have no more need of science. There will be no distinction between beauty and ugliness. There will be no curiosity, no enjoyment of the process of life. All competing pleasures will be destroyed. But always-do not forget this, Winston-always there will be the intoxication of power, constantly increasing and constantly growing subtler. Always, at every moment, there will be the thrill of victory, the sensation of trampling on an enemy who is helpless. If you want a picture of the future, imagine a boot stamping on a human face-forever.

...

... He gazed up at the enormous face. Forty years it had taken him to learn what kind of smile was hidden beneath the dark mustache. O cruel, needless misunderstanding! O stubborn, selfwilled exile from the loving breast! Two gin-scented tears trickled down the sides of his nose. But it was all right, everything was all right, the struggle was finished. He had won the victory over himself. He loved Big Brother.

OTHER ESSAYS

LAWS AS MAGIC

Laws are to the legal system what incantations are to magicians: a camouflage and a facade for the actual causes of an outcome. This is the secret that the powers-that-be in our legal system hide just as magicians hide the secrets of their tricks in order to keep and maintain their power. Unlike magic, however, this secret will and is destroying the integrity of the legal system. This is manifested by the fact that to exercise my right of Free Speech to write this essay that I must do so anonymously to avoid retribution from the protectors of Free Speech in the court system in which I practice.

Despite my varied experience in life starting from a working class background to graduating from Harvard Law thanks to the G.I. Bill, I left law school with what I now know to be a naive belief that law involves a normative set of principles from which we logically deduce solutions to legal problems. Since graduating, I have worked as a trial attorney. It is here in the trenches of the legal system that different concepts of justice and interpretations of the law are tested, fought for and against, and victory or defeat suffered all within a framework of procedural rules making the legal battlefield equal for all who come before it and where intelligence, knowledge, and reason are the weapons.

What a bunch of nonsense. The parties in a case rarely care about the law or about what is just. Each party wants a certain result, and that result must be "justice" because they want it. The legal system responds with the sham that the parties' concept of justice is worked out and meshed into social ideals in our adversarial legal structure. This bogus response works for the rich parties and their lawyers. They go about generating huge amounts of paper, leaving no stone unturned — regardless of how relevant or material it is to a case without worry of sanctions or retribution since there is no such thing as frivolous when you have the money to make anything seem possible and your desires can never be a waste of court resources.

However, for the politically powerless for whom this third branch of government is suppose to be a refuge, the last thing judges want an attorney to do for these clients is to adversarially argue anything. This makes them work and challenges their mystique of power. What really happens is that the judges quickly decide based upon their own bias, prejudices, and ethics how the case must end up and angles everything in that direction with the "law" as the veneer.

With any real-world experience at all in representing uncelebrated cases and with any sense of honesty, a novice attorney quickly learns that what a lawyer must do is pretend to be an adversary. You must argue the case up to a certain politically acceptable point so the client thinks you care about the case without challenging the latest pre-determined disposition, bias, and prejudices of the judge. This is just as true if not more so of so-called "liberal" judges because for them the law is equivalent to a religion and any attack upon it or the latest legal fad must immediately and forcefully require excommunication and suppression. The extremes that judges go to protect and hide this contradiction is inconceivable to the observer not familiar with the court system. Judges outright lie in decisions; appellate courts add further lies in order to affirm and not embarrass such a deceitful judge; judges overturn jury verdicts after weeks of trial simply because they did not like the result; appellate judges none of whom ever tried or could take to trial a case in their politically connected lives ignore such blatant disrespect for a jury by simply affirming without decision the reversal because they could not fabricate any justification for it; attorneys lose meritorious cases simply because they did not want to anger a judge by being adversarial; and judges dismiss meritorious cases simply because they did not like an adversarial attorney.

However, who would listen to such stories? Our entire judicial branch and ninety percent of our executive and legislative branch "lawmakers" are lawyers for whom the secret is the keystone of their power. They have no interest nor incentive to reveal the secret nor to ameliorate its effects. Though in reality, we are as dependent on the legal system as a person in the Middle Ages was dependent upon the Church, we Americans have this illusionary concept of ourselves as being wholly independent individuals who only need to be left alone by the legal system to survive and prosper. This is an illusion that is not shared by the rich and powerful who keep teams of lawyers on retainer to assure they keep their wealth and power.

Though this illusion is quickly erased when unfortunate circumstances result in one being involved in the legal system, it is then too late. My worst fear in court and the one that ferments the most contempt for its daily workings is that no one is more in danger of being treated unjustly than a truly innocent defendant or a truly injured victim. Such clients honestly expect that the system will protect them simply by letting it work, wherein in reality it is they and their attorney who must be the most on guard of all. As with all previous legal systems, ours would willingly and knowingly sacrifice any individual to save its power. The only difference is that instead of destroying the individual physically our system destroys the spirit, which is much worse. How long can a legal system hypocritically claiming to be based on democratic principles survive when it keeps its power purely on hidden authoritarian principles?

SEPARATION OF POWERS

As hopefully every American schoolboy and schoolgirl knows by the time they finish the eighth grade, though the writers of the United States Constitution had respect for the value of the individual, but they were also fully aware of the individual's weaknesses such as the capability for evil and tyranny. Being fully aware, both intellectually and from practical experience, that power corrupts and absolute power corrupts absolutely, they created a government system embodying a separation of powers in three branches of government: the executive, legislative, and judicial. The emphasis was not on changing human nature or idealizing it but in establishing procedures and safeguards that would not allow human nature's weaknesses to destroy it while allowing its strengths to work and foster better government.

As we go into the 21st Century, this separation of powers is nominal only and a joke. Judges are essentially legislators in which the law is whatever a judge on any particular day with any particular case decides the law is. They are appointed because of their political beliefs to enforce those political beliefs upon society through the "magic" of laws with the only significant difference between them and the legislature and the executive is that they wear black robes to work and need life tenure to do their legislating because they do not have the courage to be accountable for their work. The judicial branch along with the executive and legislature branches of government are merely mouthpieces for whatever lobbying group or bureaucrat to whom they owe the most and are incapable of any independent political or philosophical thought. No one in academia, the wealthy, nor the government has any incentive to change this situation since their power derives from the status quo, and, unfortunately, they are the only ones with the power to change it. The system is at least 100 years behind the times. The following are a few suggestions for "procedures and safeguards" that would bring the system up to date.

First, separation of powers should be brought back in modern day form: no one who is or has been a member of one of the branches of government is allowed to become a member of another branch of government. The main goal here is to prevent the ridiculous situation in which 90% of the executive, legislative, and judicial authority is held by lawyers. This situation exists because of a circular chain of causation derived from the modern situation in which the law has become the arbitrator and mediator of all disputes in our society. People cannot solve problems among themselves without a law, the lawyers create resolutions by laws that they enforce, these cause more problems, creating a need for more laws, the cycle begins anew. Though the adverse effect on society of such a situation is often discussed, the adverse effect this situation has on the legal system is completely ignored. The legal system is supposed to be an independent branch of government with its own principles. Since its powers-that-be, the judges, are just political hacks for the politicians that appointed them, sharing the same desires and goal of maintaining their power, there is no independent branch and especially no independent thought. If in fact the judicial branch were in competition with sometimes adverse principles held by independent non-lawyers and other independent sources of thought and power from another branch of government, it would either have to become and stay up-to-date or be gone. Given the need to maintain power once one is given it, I suggest that it would stay up-to-date or, if not, its elimination and replacement by the competing powers would be more than warranted. At the same time, if the other branches of government had a judicial branch that was really independent of the latest political fad that they needed it to enforce, they also may have to start thinking in terms of political ideals again and not in marketable fads.

Second, the adversarial system of litigation and trial work should be eliminated in all cases except felonies and civil actions against the government. To the extent the adversarial system developed in earlier centuries to resolve such problems as whether farmer A's cows trespassed into farmer B's garden still exists, it adds nothing but complexity to an already complex society with its sole purpose being to allow the large law firms to make a lot of money in discovery. Its advantages exist only for the wealthy who can afford the expense that it entails. For the average party forced into the judicial system, the adversarial system exists in name only. As summarized in the previous essay submitted by another writer to this web page (see Laws as Magic above), it's advantages are not available to the powerless for whom it is suppose to be a refuge. Those attorneys that are really adversaries for the powerless risk their economic, physical, and mental well-being. Most attorneys, even the very affluent who build a reputation as good attorneys by proper marketing techniques and not by legal work, do not have the ability nor training to engage in adversarial techniques in our complex society. Those that do are more often than not persecuted by jealous judges and the jealous self-marketed lawyers, who are themselves completely incapable of courageous advocacy, to the point where eventually their skill and ability is negated or turned into sour cynicism. Eliminate it! Make the judicial system be consistent with itself and have it solve problems efficiently and economically. At the same time, such a procedural change should work so that the judicial branch becomes self-sufficient for its operating funds and for enforcement of its judgments. No more excuse that the judicial branch must be cowards because it is dependent on the money and respect of others! In the cases of felonies and actions against the government, the final defense to tyranny, the adversarial system should be fine-tuned so that the best adversaries practice there and do so with pride and respect and not with apprehension as to what their courage would bring upon them.

Third, no branch of government should be allowed to be its own "ethicist." In the 1990's, ethics has become the first refuge of the scoundrel. Every politician or attorney no matter how dishonest or crooked they may be themselves accuses his adversary of unethical conduct whenever it is convenient to do so. Thus turning ethics, a noble philosophical study over two thousand years old dating to Plato's Republic and the very foundation of Western Civilization, to a joke. As anyone who has taken even a freshman introductory course into philosophical ethics knows, it requires skills and formal logical thought that are not easy nor intuitive. Both Congress and the legal profession have "ethics" committees that supposedly judge and govern the ethics of its members. These farce committees all have one thing in common: their members have no training, no education, nor any formal study in ethics. The committees therefore become purely another political tool by which the powers in control attack those not in control. In the case of state bars, the professional ethical committees are completely worthless except for ensuring that the desires of the large firms become the standards for the farcical "rules of professional conduct." Ethics committees should be run by independent, educated in critical thinking, experienced in life, philosophers trained in formal ethical thought.

What chance is there for any of the above procedures to become active in the next hundred years: zero to none. The feudal system hung around 500 years after its usefulness had vanished as our own revolutionary war proves. Our present government is a power that will maintain itself at all cost regardless of how antiquated it has become. Regardless of a good attempt by our Founding Fathers, they did not create a system that would keep pace with the times and prevent power from becoming the dominating motive for activity. Once the above reforms are initiated, they will probably be antiquated already and only become another source of inefficient power for some undeserving few.

Which leads me to my fourth reform, re-institute the Old Testament "jubilee" year. Every fifty years, all laws, government authority, and legal power is abrogated and made null and void unless re-instituted by the people. It is not worth voting anymore because there is nothing to vote upon that is meaningful: one politician is the same as the rest; and policy will be decided by the most influential lobbying group and not by any vote and definitely not by my vote. At least, once every fifty years give me something substantive to vote upon.

FOR WHOM THE BELL TOLLS

It is sad to see how successful insurers and the other powers-that-be have been in brainwashing the American public into worrying about the reputed social costs of excessive and meritless litigation. One would think that even the slightest familiarity with American history starting with the Salem witch trials continuing through the Haymarket trials onto the Los Angeles police officers trial and everything else in between would prove beyond doubt (not only a reasonable doubt) that the rich and other powers are more than able to take care of themselves and that we should be suspicious about any argument from them that there is some type of "social" threat in a procedure that sometimes hurts them. The nonsense that calls itself legal scholarship is worthless to counter these marketing ploys. Frankly, there is a Catch-22 situation that prevents any opposition because they cannot be countered unless one has had the misfortune of actually being a civil plaintiff or a criminal defendant, but in that case you have lost any credibility since everyone else — because of the propaganda — has no trust in you.

The funniest thing about the popular anti-litigation views is that it only applies to the other guy's litigation or defense and not of course to your own. I am constantly amazed by calls that I receive from conservative, potential clients living in a conservative, Simi Valley-like suburb who all of a sudden find themselves in need of a lawsuit to satisfy some injustice. They one day decide to argue a ticket with a cop and wind up arrested for disorderly conduct; they are completely indignant that their right of freedom of speech has been so violated. They lose their job after years of hard work because the boss is an idiot; they are sure that there is some right out there that has been violated. Their daughter goes to a hospital for a simple examination and almost winds up dead because the doctor is an idiot. They go into an intersection with their SUV that of course has the right-of-way when a Volvo driver busy admiring the safety features in his car runs into them because he or she also has the right of way. All these people expect that not only will they get millions for the injustice that has occurred but also that of course attorneys will be tripping over themselves to take their case on a contingency.

They are very quickly brought down to reality. Not only am I not interested in the case, but probably no one else is either since in this day and age before a conservative judge in their conservative, neo-Nazi little suburban world they are lucky to get out of there without losing money let alone making any. If their case is not the basic personal injury case but involves some type of new idea or principle or even more likely involves an idea or principle to which his Honor the judge is not familiar, does not understand, or does not like, you are now in the world of "frivolous" lawsuit and "Rule 11" sanctions. I would like to see anyone busy complaining about contingent fees or excessive litigation take on a rich insurer for years while financing the case on a contingency and stay out of bankruptcy court.

The reality of the situation is that the reason we have contingent fees and the American system of fees in which each side bears their own costs is because after centuries of experience our early jurists realized that this was the only way to assure the middle class would have some judicial power (forget about the working class, they are without hope). Given that this is an imperfect world, of course this means that some nonsense lawsuits will get by. Still, for every frivolous lawsuit that gets by, there will be thousands of social injustices that have no legal remedy. Though frivolity will sometimes win and the insurer instead of making $100 million in profits may only make $99,990,000, this is a lesser evil than the alternative. Now that we as a society are going the other way and are trying to eliminate frivolity even at the price of losing more legal remedies, the middle class is also disappearing and losing its powers. Americans, please wake up and read history again!

THE IVORY TOWER OF APPELLATE JUDGES

I have just read an appellate decision on a case that I handled in the trial level. As always, it is hard to recognize my case because the facts as stated by the appellate court have very little relation to what occurred. As any trial attorney knows, any correlation between the facts on appeal and the facts at trial are only coincidental. Why is this? Why is it so hard for appellate judges, who are outside the heat of battle of the trial court level, to apply some rationality and honesty to the issues before them? Ninety percent of the cases brought to appeal by an attorney can be reversed or affirmed depending on what judgment calls the appellate judges make by emphasizing some facts and law while ignoring others. What is this judgment that is the decisive factor but a factor usually never explained or even mentioned in the appellate decision itself?

A large part of this has to do with the natural inability of human nature to see any view or to understand any thought other than their own. Very few people are naturally empathetic. For those who are not, it requires extremely hard mental work, education, and mental discipline to become so. Even fewer engage in such a process. Trial attorneys, even if they are not concerned with empathy as a virtue but only as a means to success, must if they want to survive understand the opposing side's case or view in order to defeat it or to know they may be defeated by it. The miserable work that negates nature and develops such an understanding requires years to succeed and that success usually occurs after a painful defeat.

The vast majority of appellate judges never had this ability nor to they ever have a need to develop it. A judge, whether appointed or elected, conservative or liberal, is primarily a politician and only secondary, if at all, an attorney. They accept illusion as practically more important than substance. They got their job by understanding who the powers-that-be are and making that power happy. They worked and work within the system and are part of the system. Any mindset that would cause them to see and appreciate a view contrary to their own or outside the system and really disturb it, not just nominally or ephemerally cause a politically correct ripple, but to really have a completely contrary view is beyond their nature or they would not have gotten the judgeship.

Furthermore, this natural inability is worsened by the fact that appellate judges exemplify ivory tower philosophers spitting out ideas that have no control by reality. Their personal ideas are pure and enforceable law. They are never critiqued nor could anyone do so since there is no basis for a critique. What they say is law and is by definition correct. The only way outside of it is by rational principles of reason, logic, and ethics. However, we have rejected all such argument to have the efficiency of allowing only legal arguments. Of course, while we do this, we complain about having too many lawyers and litigation and such, but hey what the heck, hypocrisy is not a crime.

A dominant factor in appellate judgment regarding what facts or law to ignore and what to emphasize is the idea that the underlying decision on appeal must be affirmed as long as it does not contradict what they believe to be right or just. As part of their professional courtesy to fellow judges and as part of the desire to exhibit the system to be true and accurate regardless of how false and erroneous it really is, it is vitally important that judges be shown to make few mistakes. After this factor, there are probably an infinite number and variety of factors that affect appellate judgments: political and ideological views; the nationality or race of the parties or attorneys; the demeanor or style of the attorney or party; what the judge had for breakfast that day; what the judges law clerk had for breakfast that day; and so forth to name any possible view, prejudice, opinion, or bias that a human being may have.

What would be so wrong or hard in admitting this reality so that we can compensate for it? Would it not then be possible to bring the appellate system into the 20th Century (we would work on the 21st later) by such minor changes as actually having mandated basic educational requirements and qualifications for judges, competency tests, and even an independent examination board to review their performance? How about a real change such as admitting that what they are really doing is making ethical judgmental decisions and then force them to write their ethical views of the issues and parties in their decisions and to start studying, knowing, and applying ethical logic and reasoning!

THE RELIGIOUS LEFT:
LAW AS THE NEW STATE RELIGION

In reading the Goodridge decision legalizing same-sex marriages, I finally realized of what this decision and so many other politically correct decisions going all the way back to Roe v. Wade remind me - that of a preacher's sermon in a church. There is no doubt that the law is becoming, if it has not become already, the new state religion. In the same way that the previous dominant Western religions destroyed Roman Law, now, the descendent of Roman Law through permutation by Christian ideals is getting its revenge by destroying religion.

Starting in childhood and going into my early adult years, I studied different religions and the dogma and institutions they fostered, listened to their sermons, and read their beliefs. There is one element clear in all religions, that is, the essential meaninglessness of words. Any word pretty much can mean whatever the preacher, prophet, or whatever wants it to mean to a receptive audience. This includes also the very basic, simple words such as "brother", "sister", "father" or whatever. Words are used to achieve a certain goal without any attempt nor need to learn the history, initial meaning, or intentions of the use of the words and without any attempt to study or understand the ideas and background that led to the creation of the words; they are essentially used for whatever purpose the religious leader using them has in mind. The same words can be used alternatively to support peace or war, social order or disorder, logic or illogic, or whatever. Much of this was due to the fact that the basic purpose of religion is in fact an irrational goal — giving meaning to an irrational world — and to the fact that the front-line preachers of any religion are usually not educated enough nor competent enough to deal with the study of the history, logic, ethics, and rationale behind a given word's use.

Supposedly, the law is to be different. The "common law" or even the "civil law" tradition is supposed to be based on some type of logical or rational relationship to the past or at least the awareness of such a restriction and then an honest attempt to adhere to it.

If that were ever true, it is clearly not true any longer. Even as religion for many reasons is losing its meaning to individuals and failing in providing a structured social goal, to many the law is now providing their meaning in life: it is giving them hope; it is giving them remedies for perceived injustices; and it is providing a means for an acceptable social order in which every one has certain "rights." In the same way that the initial development of Western religion was seen as an alternative to the despairing power of the Roman government and empire, now Western Common Law, a direct descendant of Roman Law, is seen as a alternative and remedy for the apparent despairing and failing power of Western religion to provide hope and social order to the modern world.

Part of the process of doing this is to take words such as "due process", "equal protection", and "right" and through the use of preachers known as judges to turn them into meaningful tools for the politically powerful to create a society in their own image. As with the sermons, this is usually done by individuals who have no training, competence, or caring about the cultural, social, or historical development and the intent of these words. The four judges who joined in legalizing same sex marriages in the Goodridge case - Marshall, Cowin, Greaney, and Ireland - are probably the least competent judges at the appellate level and probably make the top ten list of incompetent judges for the whole Massachusetts court system. All of them were incompetent attorneys whose only success was to become well enough politically connected hacks to be appointed to the ultimate hack job, that of being a judge. None of them has had an original thought in their entire politically correct careers and yet have reached the point of making their own personal ethics dogma for an entire society, without ever devoting a minute of their life to a study of the concept of ethics. They have done this in the same way that the hierarchy of churches or religions issued proclamations based on "infallible" revelations.

Actually they have done it in a more dishonest and incompetent way. Organized Churches actually make dogmatic changes only after centuries of study and argument by learned people that is available and open to the public — many times the ideas behind these changes are truly difficult, subtle, and thoughtful. Case law is make by hacks with no qualifications other than they pleased some politician somewhere enough to get a hack job with the real reason behind the decision hidden in their chambers or by their worshiping law clerks to avoid the disrespect for the decision that would come with honesty.

What is someone like me who works in the trenches of the legal system to do? (A system that supposedly protects free speech but which I must criticize anonymously in order to protect my clients from being forever barred from ever again winning a case?) Should I keep the faith and pretend that there really is such a thing as "law" distinct from religion? That is what so many dissenters to these politically correct cases seem to do — stating I "respectfully dissent" to the decision no matter how dishonest it is. What a bunch of cowards. No more. I am no longer keeping up the faith or the facade. The law is what a judge on any particular day in any particular mood says the law is. From now on, I am passing this empirical truth on to my clients and the system is on its own in trying to survive, it will get no help from me.

RESPONSIBILITY AND THE LAW

Simultaneously, people are proselytizing about the legal system being a means of holding people responsible for their actions while also complaining that there is too much 'litigation.' As any honest, experienced trial attorney knows, both expressions are inaccurate. Normally, the only people held responsible for their actions are those too poor or too outcast to get out of being held responsible for their actions. The law is primarily a means for maintaining social order and stability in the economic conflict between the rich and the poor. One means by which it achieves this goal is by the social opiate of occasionally allowing income redistribution from the rich to the poor through lawsuits that are able to beat the system. Social hypocrites should realize this and stop complaining about a system that surreptitiously works to maintain their power and a class based social order.

One noticeable difference between the 9/11 attack on the United States and the Pearl Harbor attack is that despite the fact that the American casualties were about the same that absolutely no government agent or employee was held accountable in any way for the 9/11 surprise attack. After Pearl Harbor numerous government entities and employees were demoted or lost their jobs, including high-ranking officers in the Armed Forces. However, several years after the 9/11 attack, no one in any government agency has in any way suffered any reprimand or loss as a result of what was clearly a failure by government authorities to protect their citizenship. The same is true for the aftermath of the debacle in New Orleans. (I do not consider voluntarily resigning your government salaried job to then make tenfold profits writing a book or working in the private sector while keeping the government pension benefits as being held 'accountable'.)

Such lack of accountability exists throughout the state and federal government system. One would be hard-pressed to find an instance of any government employee of any rank who has lost their job because of incompetence in the last 40 years. Here in Boston, the Big Dig Highway Project has gone from an estimated cost of $2 to $4 billion to over $14 to $16 billion with the result consisting of what are supposed to be waterproof tunnels leaking and corroding within weeks not decades of their opening. Yet, not only has no one lost their job or been reprimanded, but the Massachusetts Turnpike Authority and its officials have been awarded with more power and more money to correct the problem. The government principals who made the errors in the first place simply left their jobs with large severance packages.

This lack of accountability is occurring and becoming standard procedure despite the supposed fact that we are an 'overly litigious' society that excessively tries to hold everyone accountable through 'the law.' Worthless legal academics and non-trial attorneys are either complaining about too much litigation or saying 'meritorious' litigation makes people accountable for their actions. Trial attorneys know both to be nonsense. Why is this occurring?

Any time trial results affect the power of the powers-that-be, there is an immediate correction that negates that effect. For example, the area of police misconduct civil rights law is worthless for anything except headlines every four or five years to give liberals and conservatives something about which to argue (the same is true for most civil rights law). In reality, incompetent police work, false arrests, excessive force, and outright batteries by police on civilians is a daily occurrence in even small cities and liberal states such as Massachusetts for which it is impossible to hold police accountable. There are usually only two kinds of witnesses to these events: the police and the civilian. The police stick together admitting nothing and lie with professional skill. Before a judge or jury, credibility will always go to the professional perjurer and no trial attorney would handle such a case since it is unwinnable.

If there is some type of hook that would allow for trial in a police misconduct civil rights case, there are then the very difficult legal defenses to overcome: good faith immunity and supervisory/municipal liability. Unlike every other person who has violated the civil or criminal law, the Supreme Court in its wisdom has given police the defense of 'good faith immunity'. This means that even if you can prove factually that the police have violated constitutional law, if they in 'good faith' believed they were doing the right thing, then they are not liable. This is equivalent to a defendant accused of statutory rape being able to legally defend the charge by saying that he honestly and in good faith believed that the minor was an adult. Furthermore, unlike every other employer in the United States who must face vicarious liability for the wrongful acts of its employees committed in the course of their employment (meaning that if your employee violates the law during the course of carrying out the duties of their employment, the employer as the principal is liable for this agent's actions), the Supreme Court in its wisdom has decided that government employers do not have to face this liability faced by all other employers in the world. If an individual police officer violates constitutional law, its employer government is only liable if the plaintiff can somehow also prove that there was a policy or procedure established by the government to allow such

83

unconstitutional acts, something that is further defined so strictly that it is almost impossible to establish or so expensive to establish that only the richest plaintiffs can even attempt to do so.

These factual and legal obstacles mean that the daily incompetent action of police officers in which they spend an enormous amount of taxpayer money and their time acting as bullies and punishing civilians for not treating them with 'respect' instead of rationally investigating and dealing with crime and criminals goes completely unpunished without any type of accountability. Eventually every five years or so, the police get so confident in their daily abuse of power, that they wind up shooting someone for no reason or star in a videotape beating of a civilian resulting in headlines and multimillion dollar verdicts. Of course these verdicts are not paid by the individual police officers, usually no supervisor nor anyone in authority loses their job nor loses a penny because of these cases, but the taxpayers wind up paying money to resolve the case and make it a go away so that the police can go back to their usual daily routine.

Personal injury cases are also another area in which there is no responsibility or accountability involved. Despite personal injury attorneys' constant marketing that they are concerned about victims, they really are only concerned for victims who have a case against someone with insurance or with a deep pocket. Even in such cases, the defendant who actually committed the wrong is not being held responsible in any way but simply his insurance company pays money; it suffers no loss since it always recovers whatever money that it pays from its insurance premiums and thus its enormous profits continue. The beautiful deception of personal injury law is that it does its job of maintaining social order by occasionally transferring money from the rich and powerful such as insurance companies to the claimants of lower income classes. Thus, it also serves as an opiate for the masses keeping them from revolting against the large economic disparity that exists.

For every big personal injury verdict there are a 1000 meritorious cases that have no remedy and this fact goes unnoticed by the powers-that-be that causelessly keep complaining about excessive litigation. The best control on frivolous litigation is the contingency fee agreement. No attorney in his right mind is going to take on a so-called 'frivolous case' against a large and rich government or corporate entity or insurance company on a contingent fee requiring that he finance the case for years and incur enough costs to go bankrupt. The only cases that are taken on a contingency fee are cases that have merit, and even these meritorious cases, more often than not, run up against institutional barriers and prejudice that result in their being lost or in achieving far less than what should have occurred. For every even remotely frivolous case that makes it to through the court system, there are a hundred meritorious cases that cannot be accepted and litigated because they are politically incorrect or attorneys cannot risk the financial burden required to litigate the case when it is compared to the possible financial result.

There is numerically less litigation now than there was even in the depression era pre-W.W.II period, and most of present litigation never makes it to trial. In areas where there is a small percentage increase in litigation, it is insignificant when compared to the increase in the complexity of our society. Most of any increase in certain types of litigation occurred as a result of the 1960s in which social unrest required that the legal system give more than illusionary rights to the powerless in order to maintain social order. However, as these rights are given to the powerless to act as an opiate to maintain social order, at the same time the possible permanent effect of these rights on the powers of the powers-that-be decreases. In the small amount of cases in which someone does get a large award against a power-that-be, essentially all that happens is that some income is taken from the wealthy and redistributed down to the poor to further act as an opiate to keep the economically powerless quiet and content.

The legal system establishes no responsibility for anyone and makes such lack of responsibility a standard social norm. This may be a good thing in this world that may be too complex and convoluted to hold anyone meaningfully responsible for anything anyway if such were admitted to be the case and discussed. However, this reality is not admitted but instead it is hidden behind a false facade of responsibility and the gap between theory and practice continues to undermine the viability of the legal system.

SACRIFICING FOR SOCIAL ORDER

A previous writer commented on the fact that the law and in particular civil rights law is worthless for making government officials responsible for their incompetence. However, I submit that such may not be a bad thing but may in fact be necessary to control government power through the only way that this world allows for such control: by sacrificing some of the powerless to this thirst for power.

As any experienced trial attorney knows, there is very little difference between most police officers and the criminals that they arrest. They are essentially the same type of person: however, at some point in their life, the person who becomes a police officer decided that it was easier and safer to be in the service of the government with a guaranteed pension at the end of 20 years of bullying people. The best way by which the modern concept of uniformed and military-type police departments solves crime is by taking potential criminals and giving them a salaried government job and a pension to look forward to if they restrict their criminal activity to the type approved by the government in short by making potential criminals police officers, crime is significantly reduced.

The unfortunate reality is that the most efficient and idealistic type of police force is the type that patrolled Germany and Italy in the mid-Twentieth Century making it possible for Germany to take on the world for several years of war and for Italy for a short amount of time to actually run in an organized and efficient manner. Is the price for maintaining civilian control of a militaristic-type police force the sacrificing of some poor and other outcasts to be the victims of police inefficiency and abuse? Is it possible that unsolved murders of the poor and powerless and high crime areas are the price that we pay so that the vast majority of people can live with little or no crime while also free of concern that the police will be turning their community into a police state? I submit that it may be so.

There are over 200 unsolved murders in the poor areas of Boston in the last few years. If this were true of an area such as Weston or Newton, we would be already a police state with military checkpoints and uniformed police routinely knocking down doors to solve these crimes. Constitutional safeguards would mean nothing to the politically correct who live in such places if their physical safety were required to be put at risk to protect those safeguards. Such sacrifice for the 'Constitution' is not required of them, but of those too poor, too ignorant, or too whatever to live in Newton, Weston, or the like. In such cases, constitutional safeguards must be maintained at the price of physical safety. If the police are so well-trained and efficient that they start solving crime in poor areas, they will have nothing to do and will then look to expand their efficient police powers to other areas. Freedom would then be in danger of being lost by everyone.

Maybe academics in law school should start to statistically and rationally discuss and study these issues. Not! They are too busy doing their mental masturbation of writing mindless, ivory tower law review articles.

PERSONAL MORAL CODE OF PROFESSIONAL CONDUCT

As all honest attorneys know, the professional codes of conduct enforced by state bars have nothing to do with moral concerns but only serve two purposes: a) to provide a basis for disbarment or other sanctions against any attorney challenging the accepted or politically correct paradigm for the judicial system; b) to assure that the method of practice designed to maximize billable hours and paperwork for the wealthy or politically powerful attorneys, in particular the large wealthy law firms, is the accepted paradigm for the practice of law. Thus, an honest attorney concerned with maintaining a sense of justice, fairness, and equity as a person and as an attorney needs to develop his own moral code, unless of course he's really a she, in which case he's got bigger problems to worry about. (Obviously, political correctness is not one of the facets of my personal moral code.)

You see this premise in the celebrity world, with Tom Cruise becoming a Scientologist (not to be confused with Anthropologists who are people who develop similar cosmological theories only theirs is based upon the firm rational basis of a petite fragment of skull bone of unknown origin) and Madonna adopting the kabala, lala, kabola, bona, kabbalah, whatever, moral code (among other things). You look at this and think to yourself, those Scientology guys got quite a racket going, don't they? Then you think to yourself what makes them so much better than me that they can adopt a new moral code and I cannot? Heck, I can make things up just as good or better than they can, can't I?

Then you look at your watch and notice that its time for lunch. But when you're done with lunch, you decide to start looking for a new moral code, but where in the heck are you going to find yourself a new moral code at this time of day? So of course, since you are at work, you look on Ebay but give up after spending all your money buying vintage ABBA records; then after work you drop by Walmart where, surprisingly, or not surprisingly, you find that they have no moral code.

Well, look no further, because I can, free of charge, provide you with the steps of creating your own moral code. Feel free to use it, its yours, forget about me, I'll be OK, I like standing outside in the cold, no more food for me since I am not charging for my legal work.

All you need to do is follow these 10 easy steps. There were 25 of them, but then I said to myself (a habit I need to break), "If you're going to have 25, why not keep going and include all the steps of Division I? Or better yet, why not institute a playoff system and be done with it? Having 25 sort of diminishes the accomplishments of the Top Ten, doesn't it? I mean, Boise State was undefeated this year. If they could beat Oklahoma, who's to say they couldn't have won it all? Ohio State turned out to be not that great, didn't they?"

OK, back to the steps:

Be creative. If you love penguins, then worship penguins. Send them a card, write them a poem, put them on a pedestal... heck, it might be the first time they get to look over your head. Nothing's sacred (at least not until it becomes a part of your moral code, in which case it does become sacred).

Don't be afraid to ask for money. Churches don't build themselves after all.

Exercise. Because it's good for you.

Attend as many Happy Hours as you can, because that's the best way to pick up... followers. It's the beer goggle syndrome, any moral code looks good with a few quarter (quarter, who am I kidding, they are dollar beers these days! "Yeah, I'll buy you a bucket of Buds, if you let me keep the bucket!") beers in you.

Bet on sports, because it keeps things in perspective. Just don't bet on moral codes, or you'll never make it into the Moral Code Hall of Fame.

Exercise, because it's good for you.

Don't "put up or shut up". I say "put up" and "shut up", just to be different. And because you'll be shutting up, no one will know that you are putting up, so it will be our own dirty little "secret".

Stop putting stuff in "quotations", it gets annoying after awhile.

Make Valentino Rossi one of your saints. Just because you can.

And finally, forget about holy water, incense, and fasting, they aren't healthy. Be easy on yourself. Make smoothies a required drink, allow Icons consisting only of NFL cheerleaders, perfume is allowed at services only if it is still on the woman, or better yet, require perfume to be allowed at services only if still on Jennifer Anniston. She'd make a better god than a penguin would.

LAW DAY

I always thought it was funny that Law Day in the United States is celebrated on May 1, the same day that the rest of the world celebrates International Workers Day — an international remembrance directly caused by the workings of the American Legal System. I do not know if this is a sarcastic joke by someone in the Eisenhower Administration, is a result of ignorance, or was intentional. However, as the esteemed members of the Bar gather on May 1 to congratulate themselves on the majesty of the law and their profession, in these times in which even parochial celebrations are supposed to be cross-cultural, diverse, and whatever, the esteemed members of the Bar should give some thought to the rest of the world's celebration on this our Law Day --- especially its humorous aspects in order to lighten up a little.

May 1st for a large portion of the world is a commemoration of the workers who were arrested and subsequently executed as a result of the Haymarket Riot of 1886 in my great hometown of Chicago, Illinois. Though the riot occurred on May 4, it was a continuation of labor rallies and strikes that had begun on May 1. During those four days, workers were demonstrating and striking for the absurd, politically incorrect demand of a mandatory eight hour workday. Having enough of this threat to Western Civilization, on 3 May the legal system sent in armed police to re-establish law and order resulting in the death of four workers. When armed police went to break-up another rally on May 4, someone in the crowd had the audacity to fight back and threw a bomb at the police line resulting in the death of Police Officer Mathias J. Degan. Seven men were arrested and tried for conspiracy in his murder. (Though four workers and six other policemen were killed in the riot, these deaths were caused by police "friendly fire" shooting in the dark at anything moving — an embarrassing fact not warranting public inquiry).

Since the prosecution could not offer evidence as to who threw the bomb nor connecting any defendant with the bomber, the theory of prosecution was that the defendants had published anarchist views advocating the start of the strikes and rallies that created the opportunity for the unknown bomber's acts and thus they were equally liable for the murder as co-conspirators. The trial judge using his common law powers used this theory of prosecution as a guide for his evidentiary rulings. My favorite part is Defense Counsel William Foster's closing argument. Having abandoned all hope as he entered the Inferno of closing argument (a feeling with which I am too familiar), he said to the jury:

91

If these men are to be tried . . . for advocating doctrines opposed to ideas of propriety, there is no use for me to argue the case. Let the sheriff go and erect a scaffold; let him bring eight ropes with dangling nooses at the end; let him pass them around the necks of these eight men; and let us stop this farce now.

That is what happened. All were convicted. Four of the men were hung, one committed suicide in prison, two had their sentences commuted to life. All this occurred after of course the Court of Appeals did its job of ignoring substantive error to bend over backwards to distort the law and the facts to find a way to affirm the judgment.

Unfortunately for the legal system of the 19th Century, the death penalty has one unfortunate consequence that executive tyrants have long ago learned to try to avoid, it creates martyrs. And thus we have the worldwide celebration of May Day.

As the esteemed members of the Bar gather on 1 May to congratulate themselves on a job well done, I ask that we give some thought to what the rest of the world is celebrating and ask if the modern American legal system is really any different from what it was 150 years ago and of other systems of the past 2000 years or have just the nature of the injustices it protects changed? Thanks to the protections of the law, in 2008 just as in 1886: 1% of this country's population still owns 30% to 40% of its wealth and power; 20% owns 80% to 90% thus leaving the remaining 80% to share the remaining 10% of wealth and power. Unfortunately, there are no obvious martyrs to such injustice. As the Bar celebrates its diversity of people of color, national origin, sex, sexual orientation, and whatever, do you really have any diversity of ideas or is it still governed by "ideas of propriety" instead of ideas of substance? Now as then, would it be just as willing to kill in cold blood four workers for daring to challenge its authority? My answer is "yes" to the latter; and, "propriety" rules, Dudes! - And Dudettes of course!

POLEMICS

Polemics about the 'judiciary under siege' every time someone challenges the workings of the criminal justice system again proves the hypocritical mentality of the supposed protectors of free speech that calls itself the legal profession. Instead of dealing with the substance of the free speech as the legal system constantly lectures to others, any serious criticism of it is treated as a 'siege.' On a daily basis in criminal courts across the country, police officers 'lie under oath' --- *i.e.*, commit perjury. All that happens is that evidence is tossed and a possible criminal set free on the Plebeians of society. (At least something occurred, usually I would expect a judge to rationalize around or completely ignore the lies in order to avoid suppression of evidence. Life tenure does not breed courage.)

A judiciary with life tenure accountable to no one, and these are the best options? No financial penalty nor any type of penalty to the lying police? If the judge concluded that a criminal defense attorney 'lied under oath,' no ramifications to the attorney? Maybe we can sue for civil rights violations? Suing a bunch of 'hero' police officers for aggressively trying to put a criminal in jail? That is a case that civil rights lawyers will be falling over each other to get. Not! It is much easier making fees filing boilerplate suppression motions in every criminal case. Do not forget about 'good faith immunity'; as long as the police officers in good faith believed they were acting legally, then they are as a matter of law acting legally. Try that defense next time you are in criminal court or any court with a non-police officer defendant. Maybe we can hold the police supervisor and the municipality liable for not properly training their officers that is for not properly training them how to gather evidence, they do a very good job of training them how to lie under oath given the many times they get away with it. Oh, I forgot, unlike every other principal in the world who is vicariously liable for the acts of its agents, government supervisors and principals cannot be held vicariously liable for their agent's acts. It cannot be that the life-tenured judges have any type of sympathy for their fellow government servants? Nah, can't be.

So I guess we are left with only the above two options, if there were others I am sure that our life-tenured, sophisticated judiciary constantly dealing with the fine nuances of jurisprudence would have come up with others. After all, the Massachusetts Bar Association and the Boston Bar Association are not taking turns handing Chief Justice Marshall awards every other month simply because they are a bunch of sycophants. Also, one must not think that the exclusionary rule is dogma simply because its adverse effects are felt only by the *hoi polloi*. If we had 200 unsolved murders in the last couple of years in fine, upper class towns such as Weston and Longmeadow instead of Holyoke and Dorchester/Roxbury, you should not expect that we would have armies of armed police officers knocking down doors until the crimes are stopped and solved. No, the government servants that are willing to defend the Constitution with the blood of others and to appoint judges for life would just as ardently expose the families and fortunes of the powers-that-be to the dangers of an exclusionary rule as they are to those of Holyoke. Not!

Maybe instead of treating law as dogma, the legal profession should for once honestly follow its own advice and deal with free speech criticism in substance instead of as a 'siege.'

THE MAJESTY OF THE LAW

The problems and injustices caused by resolution of social and personal disputes through trial by combat, physical conflict, or war are obvious to even the most casual observers of life or history. Therefore, throughout history, by both ancients and moderns, there have been attempts to establish an independent arbitrator, 'the law', to supposedly rationally resolve disputes among individuals or social groups in order to maintain social order. For modern Western Civilization, the law is now advocated as the solution for all social instability, for many economic ills, and has become essentially the new dominant religion of the 21st Century. Just as the injustices and harm of trial by combat are obvious, the injustices of the law go to the other extreme of being hidden and unknown to even its most intense inquisitors; are intentionally disguised and glossed over by its adherents, as with any religion; but are just as potentially destructive to both the spirit of the individual and to the stability and economics of society. Unless such unrecognized inherent injustices are recognized and confronted, resolution of disputes by law eventually will be just as destructive to civilization and the spirit of democracy as any war can be.

The present method of appointing, electing, or whatever trial judges is analogous to randomly picking someone off the street to have them referee an NBA basketball game. No matter how good intentioned, most essentially have no idea what is going on but they know that every now and then they have to make a call and thus arbitrarily do so against random players or against individuals who have somehow disrespected them. Even the most intelligent have very little preparation or understanding of their job, and all of them in order to get either appointed or elected to any type of judgeship must be and must remain a politician at heart and an apologist for the legal system as a secular religion. They base their legal career on making no enemies and the right kind and amount of friends. Anyone who actually believes in something and aggressively advocated such during their legal career would make too many enemies to ever get appointed to a judgeship. Once they are appointed or elected as judges, they remain politicians: foe to those that threaten their power, friend to those that enhance it. The concept that giving life tenure to such individuals as is done in the federal system and in many state systems will allow them to make the tough decisions is nonsense and not in anyway supported by evidence. In fact, life tenure simply causes them to be further set in their ways and beliefs by such absolute power making them accountable to no one nor to any idea other then preservation of their power. As any honest experienced trial attorney knows, trial judges just like juries make decisions based on their sympathy and empathy through their ideas of right and wrong. Even if trial judges have an idea of what may be written as law, their political instincts control their acts and decisions.

On the trial court level at least, we can give judges the benefit of a doubt and say that lies, distortions, and wrong decisions issued by them are simply the result of good intentions gone bad under the stress of having to make quick decisions of the complicated issues presented to them. On the appellate level, the situation is much worse. Appellate judges routinely, knowingly, and intentionally issue decisions containing cold-blooded lies. They are essentially a secular college of cardinals doing whatever they think necessary to maintain the facade of the religion of law. It is a disgrace that as you supposedly go up in the legal hierarchy, from municipal/district court, through superior court, and then into the 'great legal minds' of the Supremes, that the judges become more dishonest, unethical, and outright liars and con-artists. Regardless of the propaganda, though the rich and powerful may lose some battles in the legal system, they will always, without doubt, win the war eventually. Liberal or conservative, judges are all part of the same religion, union, or whatever you want to call the powers-that-be.

The legal system survives because it is seen as the only viable alternative to resolution by conflict and somehow it has so far been smart enough to take advantage of this Western view and its inherent need for social order and stability. The civil rights moment of the 60's is a perfect example. By the 1960's the legal system had for over a century formally maintained legally, established discrimination of various classes of individuals. As racial or ethnic minorities and other disenfranchised obtained previously unknown economic prosperity and power post World War II, civil disobedience and violent protest against such formal, legally maintained discrimination fermented and finally surfaced in the 60's. The United States in the 60's found itself with internally grown terrorists arguing, fighting, and dying for revolution; with many of its people attacking and burning government buildings, killing judicial officials, refusing and obstructing court orders; and with preached and practiced violation of law and violent rebellion against government throughout society. Remember Attica! Attica! And so forth. In response to this violent threat to social order and its power, the legal system started to create civil rights and constitutional protections for the disenfranchised and to break down the formal substantive and procedural legal formalities that kept people disenfranchised.

However, to hear judges and the powers-that-be of the legal system talk today, you would have the impression that somehow the legal system voluntarily and peacefully somehow changed the world by creating equal rights for all under the law! These people are either ignorant, delusional, or intentional revisionists of history for the benefit of 'the law.' Such is especially true of the Black, African-American, Hispanic, Women, and whatever groups that consider themselves to be judges from a 'minority group.' Such minorities have a substantial representation in the ranks of the judiciary now because of the honored dead who violently protested against the established power system that excluded such representation in the past. However, as any experienced trial attorney knows, such judges from 'minority' groups are routinely the most conservative, most pro-government, most pro-big business, and most pro-status-quo of any judges because they somehow have been indoctrinated into believing that the 'majesty of the law' was their savior and the savior of their people. The law is amazing in its ability to maintain this delusion for the benefit of its power.

However, as history shows, it will not be able to maintain this delusion forever with changing material and economic times. It is not clear how the surreptitious injustices of the legal system will resolve itself. Eventually, a very rich and powerful individual or organization will lose a battle in the legal system and make sure that they win the war by completely eliminating any facade of egalitarianism: no more jury trials, losers pay attorney fees and costs to the winner, eliminate any possibility of punitive damages, all lost cases are 'frivolous', and whatever. If society is wealthy enough, no one will care since the middle class and lower class cannot afford the legal system anyway for the majority of their problems so why fight to protect it or to prevent its dissolution. On the other hand, the economy may get so bad that the middle and working class will give up on the legal system in which they cannot afford to get involved anyway for resolution of their problems and will turn to the Old School alternatives: religion, family, vendettas, or a strong executive or charismatic leader to stop the nonsense. This is the way matters have worked themselves out through some parts of history, the way it worked in the German and the Fascist systems of the mid-20th Century, and there is no reason why such results cannot return if economic times get bad enough as they did in Germany so that people no longer want to play the 'majesty of the law' game.

In an attempt to avoid this, law schools and legal 'scholars' should start doing for once in their history real scholarship by first admitting the inherent injustice of any formal system of justice and to then look for alternatives and hopes for resolving such inherent injustices as they continually develop and evolve. Not much chance of such ever occurring because only politically correct ideas foster in law school not creative ideas for actually solving real life problems such as: why not explore letting ecclesiastical courts act as arbitrators when the litigants are religious; or exploring the expansion of the jury system so that juries can make legal as well as factual decisions, that is allowing them not only to make factual decisions but like judges to also in particular cases overrule the law when it considers the law to be unfair and unjust just as judges do? Democracy is becoming closed off to anyone that cannot afford a lobbyist, expanding the powers of a jury will allow individuals to least at some point in their life to have an actual say in the development of society and democracy and thus respect it.

AN EXISTENTIALIST THEORY OF JUSTICE

Existentialist thought as a philosophy has primarily served (substantively and practically) as a personal philosophy dealing with the meaninglessness of life and the moral decision of suicide. When it tries to deal with social or ethical concepts beyond the needs of the individual, it becomes primarily a means for French dudes to get laid, and it makes little sense either in theory or in practice. Such a result is predictable given its premises and conclusions that life is meaningless and that all social and ethical concepts are equal in the end. Don Juan, the Actor, and the Conqueror are all equally moral individuals when all is meaningless. However, I do not believe that this is a necessary result of existentialist thought. This is the necessary result when one faces the choice of suicide, however, once one has made the choice to live and to reject suicide, this choice makes possible an existentialist theory of social ethics or justice that must be systematically studied. It is not necessarily true that existentialist thought must accept the Conqueror, whose strength is his will to conquer, as morally or ethically equal to those whose strength is their will not to conquer. An existentialist theory of justice is possible.

Once one chooses to live, the second unavoidable realization after "I think therefore I am" is that "I think therefore I need power to continue thinking". Living requires power; though life may be gifted to us at conception without our choice, one who wants to live must get the power to continue staying alive from the moment the choice to continue living is made. An individual who is born rich or an ascetic surviving with few possessions may not need to acquire further or much power to live but regardless of how little power one needs to acquire, living does not occur naturally. If we let nature or natural law have its way, both the individual and any society of individuals would die of 'natural causes' quickly and most likely painfully and miserably. I refer to this need as 'power' or in the classical sense the 'Will to Power' because such choice of words best describes the various forms of work and effort in which human life engages in order to survive. This is true of all life. Animals and plants spend their whole existence hunting each other as food to get the power to live.

The human need for power in life goes beyond just food: humans want the power to control their lives and thus eventually, once one starts interacting with at least one other individual to form a society, the power to control the lives of other humans(whether real or imagined). Thus, having survived the absurd reality that life is meaningless, the Absurd Man must now face the absurd reality that life is meaningless and unjust. Not only will one never naturally get what one needs to live, survive, and to have some fun and passion in life, but one's attempts to live, survive, and have some fun will unavoidably be conflicting with and most likely will be threatening to someone else's attempts and need to do the same.

Furthermore, the need for power and the ability to satisfy the need for power are never in balance. A poor man who is lazy and uneducated and a captive of his vices will most likely always remain poor both materially and in spirit. However, a rich man who is lazy, ignorant, and a captive of his vices will become, with a little bit of luck, a President of the United States and rich in all things. Though hard work may get the poor out from poverty, the cost of such success will be either destroying his spirit by such hard work or the selling of his spirit to the needs of the rich. Either way the poor man has lost and sold himself to those rich in power. The only way a poor man can keep his virtues is to remain poor surrendering hope for a better material life. In short, There is no justice in life; this is not a contingent fact but a necessary fact of life. As the Good Book says, the race is not always to the swift nor the battle to the strong, but that is the way to bet.

As with suicide, there are two ways for the Absurd Man to respond.

One can respond with the 'Leap of Faith' prescribed by the first Existentialist, Soren Kierkegaard: if there is no justice in this life, believe there is justice in the next. Secular existentialists are too quick to reject this option and such quickness shows an irrational bias and prejudice that should not be present in a philosopher. Religion has faced and dealt with the injustice of life for millennia; there is no justification to reject such experienced thought outright without at least understanding or at least trying to understand its complexities and subtleties. The Christian answer is very brilliant, powerful, and has served the Western World successfully and pragmatically for two thousand years now and is best summarized in the Parable of the Workers in the Vineyard. This simple yet intense and profound parable dismisses injustice in life because love exists between God and Man. It in no way attempts to hide the true nature of God as the ultimate Power that can do as It pleases with Nature and the Man that It created. It shows justice to be a human concept; an all-powerful Being who created Nature can do whatever It wants with it. Trying to attach the term 'unjust' to such a being as God that in essence defines the natural order or divine order of existence is meaningless and exhibits only the arrogance and stupidity of humanity. Christianity offers us union with such power through God's manifesting itself by becoming human in the Person of Jesus Christ.

This is quite an amazing conceptual structure and thought. It turns the arbitrary power of God from being the source of injustice into the negation of the concept. The reward for such a Leap is incredible and it is very tempting to jump if one views it objectively. If faced with a beautiful woman who may be a bitch, a man is still very attracted to her and wants to fornicate with her as long as her beauty lasts regardless of her bitch factor. With God, you know the beauty will never fade and the union will always be real, so why not put up with the bitch factor especially when by doing so you are essentially becoming one with all of nature and humanity and thus ending all the conflict that is the source of injustice? Christianity has even developed the concept of the Holy Spirit to act essentially as a marriage counselor between God as a Man and God as the supreme Deity the Father.

Of course, the Absurd Man would protest that such a critique misses the point: accepting injustice as answer to the question of justice is the same as accepting suicide as the answer to the question of meaningless. This would be a correct critique if one were still debating the issue of meaningless and suicide. Once one accepts life, such a critique is no longer valid.

The other option is to go the opposite way and reject God and the universe He created. By rejecting such, I do not meet substituting it with another god as usually occurs. The Absurd Man instead of seeking the power to live by constantly seeking the power to live should achieve such power by constantly fighting another's seeking of such power without heightening the battle for power. We must remember that in this critique we are no longer dealing with morality or with just one individual's battle with meaningless and suicide; when thinking of social concepts such as justice and ethics, there is always at least one other person out there trying to get or to share in the same power and thus inevitably trying to defeat us or to conflict with us in our Will to Power. Even if we were to reduce ourselves to the bare essentials of life living in a village of two people with all the resources in the world, unless we die of boredom there will come a time of conflict when the other will want to take power from us or power over us. When that moment comes, the options are either to choose to be a conqueror and fight over such power or to run away, in the end these options are the same because neither change the nature of life and the choices are morally equal.

However, I submit that the Absurd Man has a third option: he can spit in the face of destiny and fight not the conqueror but the fact that the conqueror holds such power. He can in defeat spit in his Conqueror's face. In the latter situation, the Conqueror, Don Juan, and the Actor are not equals. The first cannot but relish, seek, and enjoy power over others. Though the latter also enjoy such power, their enjoyment does not necessarily come from taking power away from others but in multiplying, magnifying, and sharing it. Of course, the latter's means for power will in the end be defeated by a new or another conqueror just as in the end God will defeat all of us, but that is not the point. Having chosen life, the Absurd Man to exist as a social being must choose the path to power that is unnatural with the same passion that he chooses life. When faced with the bitch factor in a beautiful woman, the Absurd Man will see it and recognize it and reject the whole beauty as unjust. In doing so, though one passion is being lost, a greater passion is gained by the knowledge that one has at least for the moment beaten the unjust Nature of life. In this situation, the Don Juan is no longer ethically equal to the Actor but ethically worse because he does accept and uses the bitch as a source of power for him. This type of analysis I submit can be used to discern just and good individuals and acts from unjust and evil individuals and acts in an existentialist world.

Obviously, there is a need to work out the details of such an existentialist theory of justice, however, it must first be recognized that such is possible.

THE FARCE OF "NATURAL LAW"

The sad events of this year's Japanese earthquake once more show the need for humans to wake up to the reality of nature and to start basing legal and political systems on such realities instead of illusions. An earthquake is a natural phenomena that in this case killed at least 20,000 people. It damaged a nuclear reactor but this damaged reactor has killed no one. Yet, the only thing that politicians and the politically correct can talk about is the danger posed by nuclear reactors. This is ridiculous. Technology and the political and legal systems that allow it to develop and prosper have done more to create justice in the world then any ethical or philosophical systems that constantly only just talk about the need for justice.

Every year the amount of individuals killed by nature is at least 1000 times greater than the amount of individuals killed by man-made disasters yet the politically correct keep talking about nature as if it is some kind of beautiful thing that helps and fosters the development of humankind and civilization. This is a farce. The only people who have this view are those that live in their politically correct world with the security of family trust funds to back them up as they view nature from their beach house or mountain side retreats. Whatever justice and equity there are in the world is man made. We should accept this and concentrate on bringing justice and equity into the world and controlling all injustices both man made and natural and not waste time on seeking a natural order or justice based on "Natural Law". Both the political system and the legal system should accept this reality and stop dealing with principles such as Natural Law arguing that there are basic or natural concepts from which all legal systems and legal rules derive. This is nonsense. If legal systems were based on Natural Law, it would be fascism that rules the world not any type of equitable democratic principles. We have democracies because we want them and make them work. A democracy does not work simply because it is "naturally better". Throughout history, all democracies have eventually failed and became dictatorships. If we use illusions to maintain them instead of pragmatics, we will be next. We must use all tools to make democracy work and prosper and not be restricted by false illusions that "nature" will help us. It will not unless we make it help us.

As pointed out in other Essays here, the law is just as much a part of the unjust and inequitable forces that exist in the world as anything else. The powerful — be they capitalists, communist, or whatever — use the law to maintain order regardless of the nature of the order. Until we realize this hard fact and stop dealing with illusions about Natural Law, we will never be able to control the power of the law by such means as suggested in the other essays printed here

LAW AND ECONOMICS HISTORICAL ANECDOTES

The "law and economics" movement is an attempt to avoid much of the ambiguity and dishonesty in the so-called "justice system" described by other essays here by trying to put the legal system on a pragmatic foundation; justice becomes that which is economically sound policy for society. In many ways, it is the most accurate description of how legal systems work. Though legal systems claim to be dealing with an abstract concept and goal of "justice", they really only serve to maintain whatever the economic status quo is: to keep those in power in power. If the legal system can be tied to an economic result of assuring the existence of a strong and prosperous middle class such would in turn assure the existence of a strong and prosperous society, in theory, this is a good idea.

There is no chance in the foreseeable future of any state or federal court adopting any type of economic analysis as a means to create common law. Though subliminally or implicitly and maybe even unknowingly, judges are helping the rich stay rich and get richer, they are not going to admit it nor most likely do they have the ability to even analyze what they are doing from the economic perspective. However, both the proponents and opponents of law and economics theory fail to even have a realistic view of what they are dealing with and therefore make it unlikely that its potential will ever be realized and implemented in practice. A few historical anecdotes that I have always considered interesting and always a source of both amusement and sadness point out this reality.

Jesuit missionaries were well established in China by the mid-16th Century at a point when China was still ruled by an emperor and used a lunar calendar to govern its agricultural and other seasons, such as establishing the Winter Solstice which was just as important to the Chinese as getting an accurate date for the Easter, Christmas, and the Summer Solstice in the Western world. So seriously did the Chinese take this issue that they did not hesitate to employ the Jesuits along with other foreigners such as Arabs and Persians in the emperor's official bureau of astronomy. The Jesuits saw this as an opportunity to spread the influence of Catholicism and evenly worked within the emperor's bureau to show off how advanced Western astronomy was at that time compared to Chinese astronomy. Though the mathematics of the Jesuits in China was still out of date by Northwest European standards (they were still using earth-centered models of the Universe), but their mathematics and astronomy were much better than what was available in

China at the time. By 1610, many Chinese astronomers were so impressed by Jesuit mathematics that they secretly converted to Catholicism.

When the Manchus seized Beijing in 1644, the new emperors decided that year and again in 1664 to have a public tournament of solar eclipse predictions stating that whichever astronomer's predictions were the most accurate that than the entire empire would convert to their religion. The Jesuits, even while using mathematics with little algebra and no calculus that was decades behind what was available in Northern Europe, beat out all of their non-Christian competition and in 1644 were actually right on with the exact time and date of the eclipse. By all pragmatic considerations, the Chinese Empire at that point should have converted to Christianity and radically changed the course of history. Such did not happen because the Emperor came to realize that such a conversion would require that he become a monogamist and give up his concubines and similar traditions. China stayed predominantly non-Christian because emotion, in this case the simple emotion of lust, overruled economics.

Similarly, though I hate insurance companies for the thieves that they are, sometimes the statistics that they compulsively keep show a unique perspective on human nature and society such as the following. During the slave trade that legally existed until 1807 when Britain and the U.S. abolished the trade, all the slave ships were insured against casualties suffered by the cargo --- the slaves were considered cargo. As a result there are very detailed statistics available and good statistical analyses are possible of certain economic conditions on those slave ships such as casualties. The annual death rates among the slaves that were very expensive and valuable cargo in need of protection was 83 per 1,000. However the annual death rates among the crew were 230 per 1,000. Therefore, in terms of quantitative analysis, you were three times more likely to die as a crew member crossing the Atlantic on a slave ship than you were as a slave. Quantitatively and in terms of purely rational, economic choice it appears that you were better off being a slave than a freeman crew on any one of these ships. Qualitatively, of course, is a very different analysis; how to you put a value on freedom?

In one way, quantitative analysis is better and should have resulted in the Chinese emperor converting the entire nation of China to Christianity which would have radically changed the course of world history — mostly for the better. At the same time, pure quantitative analysis leads to the absurd conclusion that one is better being a slave than a free man. The upper 1% of society who were ship owners did not really care about the death rates among the crew because the crew members could be easily replaced from among the desperate lower class looking for work, the same could not be said of the expensive "cargo" being transported that insurance companies demanded be protected. Such concern had to be forced upon them by the legal system and such took centuries of strikes and confrontation, it was not something that the law easily created (The same can be said of slavery, it took a civil war to deal with that one and even then the legal system needed the violence of the 1960's to deal with the aftermath.).

Until the proponents and opponents of law and economics theory realize that they are dealing with two sides of the same coin and start working together to make that coin work as a practical currency, the potential for law and economics theory will never be realized.

TABLE OF CONTENTS "WHY TOLERATE LAW"

WHY TOLERATE LAW?

By Valeriano Diviacchi

Harvard Law School - *J.D.*

I. PROLOGUE

Initially when I started reading Brian Leiter's *Why Tolerate Religion*, my first impression was that I had found one of the rarest types of lawyers especially of the academic type: one with a sense of humor. As I continued, my impression of dark humor changed to his being factious, then he was gloating, but finally I was forced to conclude he was serious. The timid, cowardly, and fainthearted response by the American religious and legal culture in essence lamely trying to justify nonexistent toleration, "special" or otherwise, worsened the tragedy of his question and answer. In Western Technological Society, the law does not tolerate religion in any sense but a nominal one and most certainly not in any normative or pragmatic sense, the only senses that matter for either law or religion. Western Law has negated and displaced Western religion to become the only normative power in Western Civilization. The realistic question that should be asked is why tolerate law *qua* law: what principled argument is there for tolerating law with its special monopoly on violence? If this special toleration for the law is really just a categorical demand unhinged from reason and evidence then by Leiter's own reasoning, it is a religion with its own morality and demigods not entitled to this special toleration. Realistically, without Western law and Western religion giving each other special toleration as separate but equal communal normative powers, the former violent and the latter nonviolent, either is a tyrant willing to kill the innocent for power and there is no principled argument to tolerate either.

"There are some ideas so absurd that only an intellectual could believe them."
— George Orwell

I.   THE NATURE OF THE QUESTIONS

Having grown up lower working class in which the only source of hope in life was through religion, and then working my way up through military service eventually into Harvard Law School, and then 25 years of solo-attorney trial practice in the miserable trenches of the American system of injustice, I am fully aware of the power and weaknesses of both religion and law. For all but a small minority of humanity, the existential question we should ask of law and religion is why we tolerate either. Neither should have the audacity to question the other's communal authority to which neither is rationally entitled. This reality should be undisputed in Western so-called "Realist" philosophy of law and jurisprudence that supposedly recognizes two separate but equal normative powers: the law is law and not morality; morality is morality and not law. Despite such existential and legal reality, a philosopher of law Brian Leiter gives fallacious answers that have little connection to reality to his question *"why tolerate religion"* while assuming that tolerating law is a given.

In asking his question, as easily could be predicted, as is true of most academics' myopic view of life, though Leiter and his school of philosophy readily make distinctions as needed between different word meanings, wordgames, legal systems, laws, rules, philosophies of law, philosophies, moralities, obligations, principles, and much more, to him and to Western Law, they consider all religions the same and assume they can be lumped into a bound variable called "religion" they can judge and give value as the law deems necessary in its wisdom. Then, using popular cliches lacking any philosophy of language, he gives the existential attributes or values of this bound variable "religion" to be: "*categorical demands* that are unhinged from reason and evidence". Amazingly, despite philosophy of law having spent more than a hundred years unsuccessfully arguing about whether "law" is a universal, in a few pages he has no problem telling us not only the ontology of religion but doing so while leaving out its most important attribute: a communal social construct just as is law.

While Leiter digitally compresses the nature of religion to its supposed essence in order to contemplate toleration, he cannot be bothered to define and tell us in any analytic sense what he means by "tolerate".

Based on Leiter's ontology of religion, faulty logic, hidden premises, and a confusion of word meanings as necessary to reach his predetermined answer — an exemplification of jurisprudence at work — the answer to his question was also readily predictable. He answers that as a matter of *noblesse oblige* within *"limits"* of religious toleration" as decided also by law, the law should not grant religion *qua* religion any special toleration or protection but simply place it alongside any other toleration the law in its wisdom decides to give to matters or liberty of "conscience". If and how this answer is to be enforced on society and pontificating on what "liberty of conscience" entails is left for another day.

The timid, cowardly, and fainthearted response by the American religious establishment to this *Why Tolerate Religion* essay is consistent with all of their other surrenders of the past hundred years to the power of law — that is supposed to be its equal in power — thus indicating the question and the answer to be facetious and gloating at best. In Western Technological Society, the law does not tolerate religion specially or in anyway; instead, as a secular religion with its own irrational disguised morality and demigods, law has negated and displaced religion to become the only normative power in Western Civilization. Realistically, in the law's path of displacement are all other moralities or matters of conscience with the intent being to have law reach perfection as a power no longer existing as a means but as an end in itself. As admitted in some of Leiter's other essays, this path is not governed by naturalized analytical thought but by elitist sympathies pretending to be Nietzschean existentialism that are really a Hegelian world view — the ultimate enemy to any existentialist free and open society.

Leiter's question raises serious questions about the power of law that should be asked by both nonreligious and religious. Why is law allowed to pretend there is a universal thing such has "law" with nonlegal obligations — disguised morality — making categorical demands less "unhinged" from reason and evidence than the morality of a thing called "religion"? How is it that modern Western law, itself a creation from the forge of Western Religion's power struggle within itself and with secular power to live on this earth with Christian morality but not of this earth, has the audacity to question its toleration of what is supposed to be its normative equal while Western religion lacks the courage to ask likewise of its creation? How is it that Western religion, Western Civilization's communal attempt to give not only metaphysical but physical meaning to the fire of time and space in which humanity burns, has become subservient to the secular religion of law created by a minority to force their power upon the majority through a monopoly on violence? How is it that philosophy of law though neither rational, analytic, nor scientific is allowed to continue to pretend it is all three?

How is it that for modern American law school intelligentsia, elitists such as Nietzsche and their cowardly version of the existentialist view on reality, individual human life, and open society have greater value for philosophy of law as motivators then the courageous version of existentialism of an Albert Camus or Soren Kierkegaard or even of nihilism? Is it time for existentialism to step out of the shadows and create its own philosophy of law? Why tolerate law?

The answer to the last question will turn out to be relatively straightforward: there is no principled basis to tolerate law *qua* law but only because the law tolerates religion and *vice-a-versa*. If the reciprocity does not exist, no one has any obligation to tolerate either. Without such reciprocity, the dominant one is a tyrant, either a legal one in the Roman dictatorship sense or an illegal one — it does not matter, a tyrant is a tyrant to whom we owe no rational obligation to tolerate.

To contemplate these questions and to lay a foundation for an existentialist philosophy of law, one must first understand the elitist and mostly delusional history of modern philosophy of law and associated jurisprudence and the fork-in-the-road duality of existentialism in modern technological society that separates *hoi polloi* from those in its Orwellian Inner and Outer Parties such as Leiter and his colleagues. In order to understand how the law has gotten to powerful position of being able to question its tolerance of religion without expecting a reciprocal question from religion and of the significance of such power, one must have a clear realist not Realist understanding of modern philosophy of law, the history of Western Civilization, and of the particular elitist school of existentialism hidden in modern law and modern Western academia pretending to deny the pragmatic value of all morality but its own — including its fraudulent wordgame pretending that its "nonlegal obligation" has a meaning other than morality. Such an understanding must not be solely an academic understanding intended to stand and be judged solely for its aesthetic value as is the case with most academic nonscientific work including all schools of philosophy of law but must be a pragmatic one.

II. THE UNPRINCIPLED REALITY OF "PRINCIPLED" ARGUMENT

Before getting to my question of "why tolerate law", one must understand the invalid and faulty reasoning; misleading and unsound premises; hidden premises; and unprincipled basis of Leiter's *Why Tolerate Religion* so that we do not repeat them and in order to understand the seriousness of my question "why tolerate law". The incredible fact that his fallacious argument and answer are taken seriously as "principled argument" requiring lame responses exemplifies the insignificant level of normative power to which Western religion has sunk essentially making his question meaningless in any pragmatic sense because there is nothing to tolerate. Thus, there is nothing to act as a control of the law as a monopoly on violence.

After defining "principled" as "reasons for toleration ... not based on self-interest, at least not directly" and then dividing "principled arguments" into two classes of "moral" and "epistemic",[1] the substance and essence of his argument are:

1. — the law is a thing that gives religion special toleration;
2. — there is no principled basis for special toleration of religion as opposed to other matters of conscience in "Kantian" and "utilitarian" theories of morality[2];
3. — sometimes religion is epistemic, sometimes it is not[3];
4. — religion is a thing that makes "categorical demands that are unhinged from reason and evidence"[4];
5. — no thing ought to conjoin "categorical demands*"* with "unhinged from reason and evidence"[5];

Therefore,

---

[1] *Why Tolerate Religion,* at n. 9 & p. 7

[2] *Id.* pp. *7 - 10.*

[3] *Id.* pp. 10 - 14.

[4] *Id.* pp. 15 - 19.

[5] *Id.* pp. 20 -27.

6. — there is no principled argument for law to give religion special toleration[6];

7. — the law ought not give religion special toleration.[7]

Even assuming all of the premises are sound and true, neither of the conclusions logically nor rationally follow even at the simplest level of logic. They would only logically follow with hidden premises: 1) the law ought not give special consideration to any thing that conjoins "categorical demands" with "unhinged from reason and evidence"; 2) the moral and epistemic principles that Leiter considered are the only ones that matter.

The first hidden premise makes the argument invalid as obvious begging the question fallacy. Having defined religion as a thing that conjoins "categorical demands" with "unhinged from reason and evidence", this hidden premise is the same as saying, "the law ought not give special consideration to religion". Why not? Throughout the law, it gives special toleration to "ought not" conjunctions. For example, no government official ought to conjoin "negligent" with "doing their job" or "intentional" with "violation of law while doing their job" . Despite such seemingly universally agreed "ought nots", the law gives special toleration to government officials by giving them various types of immunity from such conjunctions including judges who have absolute immunity for liability for their judicial actions involving such conjunctions. Since there is no reason given for the first hidden premise requiring the law not to treat this particular "ought not" conjunction any differently than the others to whom it gives special consideration, it must be a "categorical demand unhinged from reason and evidence" and thus by his definition this hidden premise is religious — law, the religion of Western intelligentsia demanding a monopoly on violence to enforce its dogma.

The second hidden premise is irrelevant to the question; if he wants to use it, he should be principled about it and ask, "why tolerate religion pursuant to any principles I want to consider".

This is not logical or even rational argument. It is not principled argument in any sense including by his definition of "principled". It is simply reaching a predetermined conclusion by mistakenly or intentionally using invalid reasoning and changing the

---

[6] *Id.* pp. 28-34.

[7] *Id.*

meaning of words as necessary to fit the predetermined conclusion — *i.e.*, it is jurisprudence.

Now, how about the premises? Are any unsound or irrelevant to either his question or his answers? Are the meanings of the words in his premises consistently used and consistent with each other and the answer? I will examine them one-by-one:

1.   The law is a thing that gives religion special toleration. It says so in the law and thus must be nominally true, but does it in reality in any descriptive sense or other sense? If the law forces meat eaters under threat of violence to live in a society where only vegetarian food is legal, is the law being tolerant or intolerant of the meat eater? The politically correct answer for now is "intolerant". According to Christian morality abortion is baby killing, corporations are not persons, and marriage is a covenant between a man and a woman. Yet, the law requires Christians under threat of physical punishment to accept the annual killing of one million babies as legal, corporations as persons, and homosexual marriage as an enforceable covenant. So, is the law being tolerant or intolerant to Christianity? Is the politically correct answer still "intolerant"? I expect not, the answer now would be "tolerant" because the law — for the present at least — agrees with the meat eater but not with the Christian morality.

So, ignoring the nominal, realistically through reasoning naturalized to science, the special toleration granted religion under the law is: do as the law orders when you morally or religiously or in anyway disagree with what the law orders, or you will be violently punished. What is so special about this type of toleration? It is realistically no different from any other toleration granted by the law. In fact, interpretively, it is the same toleration given by a sniper acting within legally recognized rules of engagement to the target within his sights; it lets the target live until the sniper concludes an act warrants execution.

Is not the substantive difference between morality, matters or liberty of conscience, and religion that religion is not an individual construct but like the law is a social construct or community with the same morality and conscience? Is not religion morality in action? If so, is not forcing religion to accept immoral communal acts an act of intolerance? Is not the substantive difference between Western religion and political ideologies such as Marxism and even Eastern religions such as Islam, Western religion's acknowledgment of "give to Caesar what belongs to Caesar, and give to God what belongs to God"? If so, should not Caesar return the favor in more than just a nominal sense?

2. There is no principled basis for special toleration of religion as opposed to other matters of conscience in "Kantian" and "utilitarian" theories of morality. This premise is sound but only because Leiter arbitrarily and randomly decided how to define "principled"; what theories of morality to consider; and to arbitrarily fabricate classes of such theories. How are his arbitrary definitions relevant to the ultimate issue presented by the question of whether the law ought to give religion special consideration or even whether there is any — not just Kantian or utilitarian — principled basis for special toleration? Leiter defines "principled" as "reasons for toleration not based on self-interest, at least not directly". He then splits them up into "moral" and "epistemic" principles. Using his definitions, there are without doubt more principled and moral reasons for special toleration other than the only ones he considers consisting of Kant's categorical imperative and utilitarianism — these are just the present fad theories of morality among academics but they are definitely not the only ones.

Morality is simply a system through which a person determines right and wrong conduct. By his reference to the United States and Canadian constitutions,[8] it seems Leiter is contemplating law in a democracy, republic, or other form of free and open society. So, should we not consider the theories of morality held by *hoi polloi*; after all, the law is not a private club for the powerful and their intelligentsia trying to create a world in their image, right?

In a free and open society, there are millions of "principled" reasons for special toleration of religion. If one is a moral subjectivist, there are as many theories of morality as there are people. According to Gallup, 89% of Americans believe in God.[9] There are hundreds of millions of individuals in the free and open societies of the Western world whose subjective moral theory says religion is entitled to special toleration as a virtue in life good for all of humanity because it gives hope that humans and their dogs will find happiness in another life. Divine command theory is a non-subjective moral theory held by hundreds of millions in Western free and open society.

---

[8] *Id.* pp. 1, 2, 14, 32.

[9] http://www.gallup.com/poll/193271/americans-believe-god.aspx

God says religion is entitled to special toleration thus as a matter of principle it is. Since Leiter is sitting in judgment of religion to determine if it is morally worthy of special toleration, as a matter of principle, should he not employ the religious virtue of empathy and view religion from the perspective of religion to see if religion provides a principled basis for special toleration — especially in a supposed free and open society? According to the *Summa Theologica* of Thomas Aquinas and most of Christian moral philosophy, religion is a special higher virtue and morality. All other virtues and morality deal with human will, not ability. A person can be virtuous and moral by good intentions though they lack the ability to act upon them. *"Cum dilectione hominum et odio vitiorum"* (Love the sinner but hate the sin). — St. Augustine. His Letter 211 at 424. This is not enough for the virtue of religion. It requires acts actually done for the greater glory of God, thus as a special virtue requiring communal action, it requires special toleration.

Of course, Leiter would consider the above religious theories of morality to be nonsense and as begging the question presented. For him, it is dogmatically obvious the law cannot allow religion to decide whether or not it gets special toleration, though he has no problem with the law deciding on its own that it will get special toleration for its monopoly on violence. He ignores Christian morality despite the historical fact of Western law's assumption, some would say hijacking, of Christian theories and concepts of morality making Western law the unique normative force it is in the Western world: for example, the law assuming (or hijacking) the Sermon on the Mount and Beatitudes that forced the law to give up such legalities as chattel slavery for the first time in human history. Without its foundation in Christian morality, Western law would not have the normative authority to now challenge the Christian morality it assumed or hijacked.

My arguments showing there are other available moralities providing the principled basis Leiter seeks is nonsense but not simply because Leiter says so. He wanted a "principled" basis for special toleration, one defined as not based on self-interest at least not directly, and I have listed some for him and could get more through numerous options in subjectivist and religious principles of morality even through secular ones such as Pragmatism — according to William James, "[o]n pragmatistic principles, if the hypothesis of God works satisfactorily in the widest sense of the word, it is true."[10] However, none of them would matter. The reality is that Leiter does not want to find any and asked his question never expecting to find a principled basis as he defined "principled". It is nonsense because morality is nonsense as Leiter has stated in his other writings: "... *moral* obligations – [that] do not really exist: when we speak of moral 'obligations' (or 'rights' or 'duties') we are expressing certain attitudes, often very intense and insistent attitudes, about what we feel other people should or should not do."[11] All moralities, including religious, Kantian, and utilitarian, eventually come down to some form of self-interest. As Leiter's beloved Nietzsche has established, in relation to the social constructs that are law and religion, "morality" is simply a means to hide one's will to power. This is consistent with the reality of the natural law of the universe: "might makes right" (I have no idea in what delusional reality Natural Law theorists live in) and consistent with the nature of the pure God of the ontological proof. As George Orwell said, "God is Power". As the reason there is something instead of nothing, God can do whatever He wants with His reality. All is self-interest; even religious saints are saints because they want to go to heaven.

Once one defines "principled" as not involving self-interest, the definition can be rationally used to deny there is a principled basis for special toleration for anything — religion or the law.

All morality is self-interest and therefore there will never be a "principled" basis for special toleration of religion as Leiter defines "principled". By fabricating this definition, he was setting his reasoning up for the answer he wanted. As I will contemplate in the next section, to the extent "morality" is a meaningful word, it is a metaphysically real one about which I cannot talk or a private language whose translation is an issue behind the scope of this essay.

Regardless, morality is not relevant to my question and should not have been relevant to Leiter's question. Defining "principled" as "not based on self-interest" and then splitting it up into "moral" and "epistemic" classes guarantees we will never find any principled basis for anything including no principled basis for special toleration of religion nor of the law.

---

[10] William James. "Pragmatism and Religion". *Lecture 8 in Pragmatism: A new name for some old ways of thinking.* New York: Longman Green and Co (1907): 105-116.

[11] Brian Leiter. *The Role of Judges in Democracies: A Realistic View.* pp. 2-3.

3.   Sometimes religion is epistemic, sometimes it is not. This is a sound statement of everything in life. Seeking an epistemic "principled" basis for special toleration of religion is also nonsense unless one admits that knowledge of God is special knowledge — which Leiter does not and will never admit.

4.   Religion is a thing that makes "categorical demands that are unhinged from reason and evidence". What categorical demands? Such as "love your neighbor as yourself"; "blessed are the poor in spirit for theirs is the kingdom of heaven"; "blessed are they that hunger and thirst after justice for they shall have their fill"; "blessed are the merciful for they shall obtain mercy"; "blessed are the clean of heart for they shall see God"; "blessed are the peacemakers for they shall be called the children of God"; "blessed are they that suffer persecution for justice sake, for theirs is the kingdom of heaven"; and other Beatitudes and Sermons.

Are these really "categorical" with no exceptions tied to reason or evidence? If so, how is Leiter able to descriptively accuse religion of hypocrisy between its categorical demands and the exceptions granted by religion in action? Without doubt the above quoted Christian demands are unhinged from reason and evidence, but is that not a good thing? If we were to hinge them to reason and experience they would convert: to the golden rule of "he who owns the gold makes the rules"; "might makes right"; "every rat for himself"; and "there are those with loaded guns and those who dig".

Unhinged from what "reason and evidence"? What he really means is "reason and evidence" not naturalized to the reason and evidence of science.

Before binding such values to the variable that is religion in his reasoning, I would think he should at least have the "principled" integrity to read the philosophical reasoning and evidence of an analytical philosopher such as Thomas Aquinas or similar Scholastic analytical philosophers and theologians upon whom much of the Renaissance and the Enlightenment was based including the rise of science, instead of intentionally limiting argument to the usual suspects and Nietzsche. What about the "ontological proof" that even in the post-modern world of philosophy has yet to be decisively refuted. What evidence is there on the question of "why is there something instead of nothing" that even science has given up on.[12] What Leiter really means in this premise is "categorical demands that are unhinged from reason and evidence with which I agree".

What about the historical evidence? Western religion as a historical fact has helped human progress much more than the law ever has. In history, law has never been on the right side of history because it has never been a historical force. It is simply an interlude between periods of lawlessness after which the lawless winners become the law and force upon the losers as law what were "nonlegal" moral obligations. At least religion throughout history until recently existed as a normative historical physical force both during interludes of lawfulness and in periods of lawlessness when law was nowhere to be found.

The legal obligations of American law started with an armed revolution by a minority consisting of mobs of fanatical tax evaders, bootleggers, gunman, terrorists, and other criminal mobs against the majority loyalists and their law. If not for the hope in some of the "Founding Fathers" criminal mob of morality derived from religious obligations such as "all men are created equal, that they are endowed by their Creator with certain unalienable Rights, that among these are Life, Liberty and the pursuit of Happiness" and so forth, we might as well call ourselves United Mob Island. If the Legal Positivist Rules of Recognition, Rules of Change, and Rules of Adjudication were left to work on their own, we would still have chattel slavery in Western Civilization. It was Christian morality making its "tastes" powerful in Western Civilization that made and makes Western law a unique power in history and at present — though maybe not in the future since according to Leiter Western law need not give Western religion special toleration.

Regardless, I will assume as Leiter does that scientific "reason and evidence" is the true and only reason and evidence that matters. Though Realism, Real Positivism, and almost all other modern schools in the philosophy of law want to be a "science of law", one will find throughout their writings as is found with Leiter, terms such as "common sense", "intuitive", "obviously true", "any educated person would know", "as understood in other domains", "ordinary standards", and so forth indicating one has reached a dead-end in reasoning or one wants to start a chain of reasoning to a specific conclusion but lacks the foundation premise upon which to start. Though schools of

---

[12] *See generally,* Jim Holt. "Why Does the World Exist?: An Existential Detective Story".

philosophy of law very much want to be a science of law, this is a very unscientific reasoning process and is a wordgame anyone educated or uneducated can play with or without any sense. Strictly speaking in philosophy of language terms, when you reach a point in reasoning requiring the use of words such as this you have reached a point "whereof one cannot speak, thereof one must be silent"; however, no one ever is. This is especially true when Leiter and others use the word "common-sense" to describe their reasoning. "Common sense is not so common". — Voltaire.

I am not saying that scientists would never use such words as "common sense" and similar attempts to avoid reasoned premises. In fact, they probably care less about philosophy of language than almost any other area of thought and even less than they care about philosophy of science. Except for the heuristic limitations of Ockham's Razor, scientists will use whatever and any words necessary to successfully solve a problem in a predictive sense; that is to predict the future given what the past was and the present is. What a scientist cannot do is pretend that scientific words have any evaluative or perspective normative meaning: state what "ought" to be. Scientists can play with the semantics and treat an "ought" statement as shorthand for an action that "is". For example, one can say that when dropping a rock from my hand from a tall building on earth, its acceleration due to gravity "is" 9.8 m/s/s, thus after eight seconds its velocity "ought" to be 78.4 m/s. However, the "is" and the "ought" are being used in the same non-normative "is" sense. The physicist saying what velocity ought to be is not making an evaluative or perspective normative judgement of the velocity but simply stating what will be the empirical "is" measurement of that velocity.

Science makes no "*categorical demands* that are unhinged from reason and evidence" because it makes no categorical demands and only cares about reason or evidence when necessary to achieve predictive value; otherwise, it is willing to dump both or either as necessary to achieve a pragmatic truth distinct from any normative meaning. As described by modern philosophers of science and scientists, science is not even limited to reason and evidence for achieving its purposes but often begins with creative, theoretic anarchy, and through techniques such as zeta function regularization scientists are even willing to play with the meanings of numbers in order to give predictive pragmatic meaning to their wordgames. "The true sign of intelligence is not knowledge but imagination". — Albert Einstein. "Science is an essentially anarchic enterprise: theoretical anarchism is more humanitarian and more likely to encourage progress than its law-and-order alternatives." — Paul Karl Feyerabend.[13] As one of Leiter's often cited philosopher of science Willard Van Orman Quine stated: "[p]hysical objects are conceptually imported into the situation as convenient intermediaries -- not by definition in terms of experience, but simply as irreducible posits comparable, epistemologically, to the gods of Homer. ... But in point of epistemological footing the physical objects and the gods differ only in degree and not in kind. ... The myth of physical objects is epistemologically superior to most in that it has proved more efficacious than other myths as a device for working a manageable structure into the flux of experience."[14]

It is to scientific "reason and evidence" that Leiter wants all categorical demands hinged. That is, all demands are to be hinged to the reason and evidence that does not care whether it exists in the United States or North Korea; in a fascist, communist, Stalinist, democratic, free, republican, or tyranny state; in a concentration camp or in a free and open society; or anywhere as long as its words have predictive meaning and are allowed to reach a pragmatic truth without normative meaning. Apparently, he does. How is this categorical demand of amorality by Leiter that everything be naturalized to science in any way hinged to reason and evidence, particularly historical evidence? If not, is it his religion? Given the reality of historical evidence, if anyone or thing is going to have a monopoly on violence over me and my community as does the law now and as naturalized law would, as a matter of my will to power as his beloved Nietzsche would say, should I not want it counterbalanced by an equal but separate normative nonviolent power — at least for pragmatic reasons?

5. — No thing ought to conjoin "categorical demands" with "unhinged from reason and evidence". Again Leiter is playing with the meaning of words here as he did most clearly in the previous premise but did to some extent in all of them. What he really means is that "no thing ought to conjoin 'categorical demands with which he disagrees'"; "unhinged from reason and evidence with which I agree"; or "be hinged to reason and evidence with which I disagree". He has no problem with law making a

_____

[13] *See generally,* Norwood Russell Hanson. "Patterns of Discovery: An Inquiry into the Conceptual Foundations of Science". Thomas S. Kuhn. "The Structure of Scientific Revolutions".

[14] Willard Van Orman Quine. *Two Dogmas of Empiricism.*

categorical demand unhinged from reason and evidence for a necessary unchecked monopoly on violence to enforce its dogma.

6. — <u>There is no principled argument for law to give religion special toleration.</u> This is an invalid conclusion. The only conclusion that validly follows from his premises is that none of the usual suspects and evidence he cites have a principled argument. There are libraries of principled argument and evidence out there for law to give religion special toleration if one actually wants to find them varying from Scholastic philosophers such as Aquinas on to pragmatic philosophers such as William James and to all of history. This is an invalid, predetermined conclusion that is more jurisprudence than principled thought.

7. — <u>The law ought not give religion special toleration.</u> This is an invalid, predetermined conclusion even assuming the law does give religion special toleration in anything but a nominal sense. It is a normative "ought" statement that logically follows from none of his mixed descriptive, interpretative, predictive, and mixture of "is" meanings for words changed as necessary to reach this conclusion. This is the unprincipled basis by which philosophy of law argues and the technique by which jurisprudence hides its morality as "nonlegal obligation".

Leiter's "principled" reasoning that he defines as not based on "self-interest" is entirely based on self-interest. Though Leiter's argument and answer are logically invalid and really not even reasoning let alone "principled" reasoning, what Leiter as a philosopher of law and law professor has given us by his question and answer is the reality of jurisprudence. Even Leiter admits such in some of his writings such as *The Truth is Terrible; American Legal Realism; In Praise of Realism (And Against 'Nonsense' Jurisprudence)*; and *The Roles of Judges in Democracies: A Realistic View.* In the former he is not referring to his nonsense jurisprudence; in the last one, it is so entitled though it is not very realistic as it too assumes the law's monopoly on violence is a given to be absolutely tolerated with no consideration of the effects of such a monopoly on a free and open society. As with Leiter, judges and other law givers view the facts, then based on their beliefs, assumptions, intuitions, and personal or universal prejudices and bias and outright bigotries decide an answer. They then go on to use or fabricate facts, word meanings, and wordgames as necessary to justify their predetermined answer they then call "law". Realistically, based on my 25 years as a trial attorney handling about a thousand cases in the miserable trenches of the legal system, a world never experienced by Leiter because it is unclean, what Leiter's question and deceptive irrational process to his answer show us is how jurisprudence reasons — that is, how judges and other lawgivers think.

Why tolerate law?

III.   THE PRINCIPLED REALITY OF PRINCIPLED ARGUMENT

As I try to answer my question "why tolerant law", unlike Leiter, I will be up-front as to what I am doing. I will only consider descriptive, normative, and pragmatic meanings as relevant because none other are. The descriptive fact that creates my rational or irrational concern, belief, or whatever you want to call it that begins my chain of normative reasoning is the law's unchecked and uncontrollable by anyone but itself monopoly on violence to enforce itself. I do not like violence; no one should be entitled to use violence on me nor my community without good reason; and most definitely no one or thing should have a monopoly on violence over me or my community. The sound historical evidence is that such a monopoly leads to humanity destroying itself through tyranny; I do not want anyone or thing having a monopoly of violence over my life and community — including God, but I have no other option with him; hopefully I do have options with the law. I am seeking those options; my question is normative. I want to know what ought to be. The truth of my answer is to be pragmatic: making what ought to be workable so that I can live life without the law (or religion) destroying me and my community. So, in essence, I am not looking for "principled" argument for tolerating law as Leiter defined "principled" since that was a joke; he only made that up knowing that he would never find any. As a matter of self-interest, I want to find a normative and pragmatic argument for special toleration of the categorical demand unhinged from reason and evidence of law *qua* law having a monopoly on violence. If the only reason for such toleration is to avoid its physical violence upon me, it is time to look for other options.

In this writing I will use the assumptions made by Leiter that there are values for a bound variable in reality called "law", "religion", and "toleration".

126

Eventually if not in this essay but in other writings, I will hopefully get to contemplate whether or not there really are such universals. It may be there are only particular laws and worse: no competent or incompetent attorney has a serious clue as to what they are; clients do not care what they are; and judges only care to the extent they can or cannot get away with execution upon any particular law. It may be there are only particular religions: Christianity, Islam, Aztec, Buddhism, so forth, that at best can be divided into Western and Eastern with significant overlap such as between Christianity and Buddhism.

The material attribute for a religion for the question at issue is whether it is not simply a matter of conscience but a communal morality of action that recognizes a necessary separation between "give to Caesar what belongs to Caesar, and give to God what belongs to God".

In asking why tolerate law, it is important not to repeat the logic errors and what may be intentional sleight-of-hand with meanings and logic used by Leiter to answer his question of why tolerate religion that allowed him to use unsound and hidden premises and invalid reasoning to reach a predetermined conclusion.

The use of language is crucial to any morality or legal system as it is to any religion. In my reasoning and in any philosophical reasoning on law and religion, there needs to be an understanding or at least an agreement as to the meanings of the words we will be using for this purpose. Specifically in this essay, we need an understanding or agreement on the meanings of "tolerate", "law", and "religion" and of the wordgame "why tolerate law"? This requires some understanding of the meaning of words. What is language? More specifically, what is the meaning of a word in language? What is the meaning of meaning? Is it meaningful to contemplate language using language? If so, to what extent is such contemplation meaningful? What is the relationship between words and truth, if any? Are science and its pragmatic truths the king of the mountain to which all else must be naturalized? These are serious questions whose answers result in paradigm shifts in any philosophy of anything, philosophy of law and morality included, and even cast doubt on whether "philosophy" is anything other than an analytic contemplation of language thus making philosophy of law, morality, metaphysics, and everything seeking non-pragmatic truth rationally meaningless wordgames.[15]

---

[15] *See generally*, Ludwig Wittgenstein. "Philosophical Investigations".

Luckily, philosophies of law and any attempt by its preachers such as Leiter to engage in discussion of morality are extremely sophomoric as philosophy and do not ask the important analytical questions about language before they start their pontificating, so we do not need to get into great analytical detail on a philosophical contemplation of language nor into any of its major paradoxes. However, we must have a basic understanding of how language is used and abused relevant to the questions at issue of "why tolerate religion" and "why tolerate law". As I stated previously, any philosophical use of words such as "common sense", "intuitive", "obviously true", "any educated person would know", "as understood in other domains", "ordinary standards", and so forth indicate one has reached a dead-end in reasoning or one wants to start a chain of reasoning to a specific conclusion but lacks the foundation premise upon which to start. In philosophy of language analysis, when you reach a point in your reasoning requiring you to use words such as this you have reached a point "whereof one cannot speak, thereof one must be silent"; however, no one ever is silent but I will try to be.

A.   Philosophy of Language Relevant to the Question

The meaning of a word either is a "thing-in-itself" existing independent of our use of the word or is dependent on our use of it.

In the former, my question would involve asking whether there is true "law" or "religion" that I must tolerate in the same way that I must tolerate my existence or in the same way that Christians must follow the true God.

In the latter, law and religion are social constructs tied to experience at one end and to theory at another end.

The former concept of meaning is called metaphysical realism and is completely absent from mainstream philosophy of law (philosopher of law Michael Moore is the only one I know of) and secular morality. It is absent for dogmatic reasons and not because of any rational proof making it unsound or invalid. A majority of professional mathematicians — the purest of logical minds — are metaphysical realists who believe numbers are just as real or more real than sense experience and they "discover" numbers in their reasoning in the same way that one discovers a stone.[16] Some of the greatest logical minds of the 20th Century were metaphysical realists such as Kurt Godel, Erwin Schrödinger (in his later years), and Sir Roger Penrose. Examples of everyday words that appear to have metaphysically real meanings independent of their use are words such as "I", "consciousness", and either the Cartesian or existentialist version of thought ("I think therefore I am"; "I am therefore I think" or "existence precedes essence"). These common words seem to have a true meaning as things-in-themselves in the world that are discovered and guide our actions and dealings in the world everywhere and anywhere in all possible worlds in which we exist, they are not contingent on social or even private use. In does not matter these words cannot be defined other than by reference to themselves nor refuted and thus logically should be meaningless since they cannot be interpreted either by the user privately or publicly; they mean existence and necessarily mean so in all possible worlds.

Without doubt, Leiter is not a metaphysical realist, nor am I. If he were, he would have phrased his question as "why tolerate false religion" or "why not just tolerate true religion". These are questions that he not only would never ask but that no lawyer in Western legal culture would ever think of asking as a meaningful question. With due respect to the truly great minds who are metaphysical realists, I am not a metaphysical realist because I agree with Wittgenstein that "[t]he limits of my language means the limits of my world" and thus "whereof one cannot speak, thereof one must be silent". I am willing to be silent about it. Any questions that may imply or implicate metaphysical realism such as "what is the meaning of 'meaning'"; "how can we use words of unknown meaning to contemplate meaning"; the private language argument; and the rule following paradox are irrelevant to the question at hand since no one who is reading this, if anyone, will be a metaphysical realist. Therefore, instead of asking "why tolerate [true] [or] [false] law", I also only ask "why tolerate law".

So, for pragmatic simplicity, I will accept that the meanings of words are dependent on their use and their usefulness to that use. This does not make all words arbitrary and random creations. A language or wordgame is a fabric of intertwined words — a "social construct" is the present popular phrase — that must at some point even if only at the periphery have some contact with factual sense experience or empirical

---

[16] Jim Holt. "Why Does the World Exist?: An Existential Detective Story" at p. 171 *et seq.*

observation, but language is not completely reducible to sense experience or empirical observation. Language is laden with theory that often decides what facts we experience, observe, and use. Such attributes are true of all language even our Technological Society's beloved scientific language.[17] "Whether you can observe a thing or not depends on the theory which you use. It is the theory which decides what can be observed." — Albert Einstein.

Forgetting to anchor a language to both ends, to fact and to theory, makes it lose its meaning but not its power; in fact, in many ways both in law and in religion, language becomes more powerful as it becomes more meaningless. Both the tragedy and comedy of such reality are readily apparent everywhere around us at the modern world constantly arguing about "social constructs" as if they can be randomly and arbitrarily changed without concern for facts or pragmatics. The power of meaningless words is obvious in the last hundred years of writings in the philosophy of law. The most obvious example is the wordgame in which some philosophers of law pretend there is other than just a nominal difference between "moral" obligations and "nonlegal" obligations in the philosophy of law.

Making the meaning of words be their use creates sets of meanings whose quantity and whose set members increase as necessary for academia to justify its daily generating of libraries of verbiage: nominal, legal, predictive, pragmatic, normative, descriptive, epistemic, interpretative, hermeneutical, deontological, consequential, and much more that I cannot remember for the moment and do not want to spend time trying to remember or looking up. It is at this point that philosophy of language and analytic philosophy in particular finds its meaning in life. "Philosophy is a battle against the bewitchment of our intelligence by means of language." — Ludwig Wittgenstein.

In dealing with these various uses, there is almost no limit to what meanings can be created. Except for predictive meanings and wordgames such as science, none will have a useful meaning for the word "true" or "truth" that can be falsified; so it does not matter pragmatically whether any of these meanings have any contact with sense experience except for contact with other words. "'When I use a word,' Humpty Dumpty said in rather a scornful tone, 'it means just what I choose it to mean — neither more nor less'."[18] The only limitation is their usefulness to the use to which the words are being

---

[17] *See* note 13 *supra*.

[18] "Through the Looking Glass", by Lewis Carroll

put. If the same word has different uses, it will have different meanings. For example, "wave" has multiple different meanings varying from use at the beach to use in quantum physics. If different words have the same use or usefulness, they will have the same meaning. "A rose by any other name would smell as sweet". This process is often called wordgames. This concept does not mean however that the same word used in one wordgame can be moved to a different wordgame and retain in its meaning by assumption; it retains its meaning if it retains its use and usefulness. Also, words cannot change meaning within their usefulness. So, for example one cannot take the words of a descriptive wordgame supposedly stating "what is" then to state an interpretative conclusion stating the relationship between "what is" using the same words by assuming they will retain the same meaning.

An example of the latter intertwining is Leiter's wordplay with "tolerate" and "toleration" that he fails either inadvertently or intentionally to define analytically despite the fact it is the substance of his question and argument — *Why Tolerate Religion.* Instead, as a judge would, he plays with these words as necessary to reach his pre-determined answer. At some points he uses "toleration" and "tolerate" to describe how persons treat each other, *i.e.,* they do not act adversely against neighbors who are empirically different from themselves. The words are then used in an interpretive and hermeneutical sense, *i.e.,* in order for persons to tolerate each other they cannot be indifferent to each other. (This interpretation is false. I have dealt with many cold-blooded killers who are indifferent to my existence but tolerate it anyway until the day they randomly or for a reason may decide to stop tolerating it.) Finally, it becomes normative, *i.e.,* we ought not give special toleration to religion.[19]

As you can infer already, much of these wordgames are arbitrary creations and often overlap in practice for aesthetic reasons — for words or wordgames with no predictive value, aesthetic value is as good a value as any other. Nothing is more aesthetically pleasuring to the rational mind than listening to itself talk or reading its words. This is true of even the simplest of descriptive meanings. As any reasonably experienced trial attorney will tell you, if you ask a hundred people to describe the same event, you will get a hundred different descriptions because each person's interpretation of the event affects what they will describe — and what they see in the first place. This

---

[19] *Why Tolerate Religion?* pp. 2-3, 32-33.

is one of the reasons that led the philosopher Willard Van Quine to describe knowledge as a "man-made fabric which impinges on experience only along the edges".[20]

There are at least two relevant wordgames however that are logically independent and must not be allowed to overlap in meaning even for aesthetic reasons if you are to have a logical contemplation on why tolerant anything: "is" statements and "ought" statements. The nature of this logical reality is known by names such as "is-ought", "open question", Hume's Law, or Hume's Guillotine named after the philosopher David Hume who described it best and as follows:

> In every system of morality, which I have hitherto met with, I have always remarked, that the author proceeds for some time in the ordinary way of reasoning, and establishes the being of a God, or makes observations concerning human affairs; when of a sudden I am surprised to find, that instead of the usual copulations of propositions, is, and is not, I meet with no proposition that is not connected with an ought, or an ought not. This change is imperceptible; but is however, of the last consequence. For as this ought, or ought not, expresses some new relation or affirmation, 'tis necessary that it should be observed and explained; and at the same time that a reason should be given, for what seems altogether inconceivable, how this new relation can be a deduction from others, which are entirely different from it. But as authors do not commonly use this precaution, I shall presume to recommend it to the readers; and am persuaded, that this small attention would subvert all the vulgar systems of morality, and let us see, that the distinction of vice and virtue is not founded merely on the relations of objects, nor is perceived by reason.
> *A Treatise of Human Nature* (1739).

Despite centuries old Hume's Law and a century of modern philosophy of language, all modern schools of philosophy of law without explanation and without any attempt at analytical justification assume they can infer from statements about experience, from what "is", to evaluative or perspective normative statements, to what "ought" to be. Jurisprudence has gotten away with such dogma for millennia. One can play as many wordgames as one wants such as calling "ought" statements nonlegal obligations or economics instead of morality, but no matter how you change your syntax or semantics, there is no way to deduce nor induce from predictive, descriptive, epistemic, interpretative/hermeneutical, or any other fabricated categories of statements

---

[20] "Two Dogmas of Empiricism".

of what "is" to conclusions expressing a new relation of an evaluative or perspective normative "ought". Logically and rationally, no matter how well hidden the meanings may be by the fabrication of words to hide what is going on, one can only go from evidence of "is" statements to other "is" statements and from "ought" statements to other "ought" statements.

Eventually, to avoid an infinite chain of ought statements to justify one's evaluative or perspective normative statements of what ought to be, one must start at the beginning by foundation premises relying on beliefs, assumptions, and intuitions using words as Leiter does in his essays such as "common sense", "intuitive", "obviously true", "any educated person would know", "as understood in other domains", "ordinary standards", and so forth to hide the transition from "is" to "ought". All rational normative argument is founded upon and begins with irrationality. In law and economics, the sleight-of-hand is done by calling the "ought" statements economics. In Legal Positivism, the switch is done by calling them "non-moral obligations". These are all attempts to avoid Hume's Law.

To the extent "morality" is a meaningful word and wordgame, it is either as Leiter states a rational structure of personal "tastes" or a metaphysically real one about which I cannot talk or a private language whose translation is an issue behind the scope of this essay. Regardless of which it is, it is irrelevant to my question.

Leiter, as do most academics, jumps around without acknowledging the change in meanings of his words hoping no one will notice as necessary to reach a predetermined result. He starts out concerned with the legal meaning of his question in the wordgame of the law: its "special treatment" in the "American and Canadian constitutional law". At that point, his question should have been phrased: "why tolerate religion in a legal sense". This is a boring question that is meaningless in any sense but nominal giving an answer that cannot be refuted: because the law says so. Similarly, if I phrase my question as "why tolerate the law in a legal sense", it too would answer itself, cannot be refuted, and thus would be meaningless except nominally.

In both our questions, we are really asking for a normative answer. He is asking whether the law ought to give religion special toleration. I am asking whether religion or anyone ought to allow law a special monopoly on violence.

After ignoring the legal meaning of his question, Leiter goes on to various forms of wordgames — in a very unscientific manner though he wants everything to be naturalized to science — involving and varying from descriptive, interpretive, and normative or moral meanings through epistemic meanings (all of which he calls principles) and ends with what are predetermined disguised normative or morality statements as answers to his question. He starts out with meaning in a legal sense and through a thought process using different meanings ends with normative meaning: the law ought not single out religion for special protection. Can he switch from initial meaning to other meanings to a completely different meaning from words taken from completely different wordgames? No, this is an invalid fallacious combination of different meanings and wordgames to give the appearance of valid argument and contradicts the entire concept of meanings being dependent on their use and usefulness to a given wordgame in which the words are used.

To what use and wordgames are my words "law", "religion", and "tolerate" useful?

1. *What is "law" relevant to the toleration being questioned?*

Modern philosophers of law have been arguing for about a hundred years over the meaning of "law" and have fabricated all sorts of aesthetically pleasing wordgames for it. (In classical philosophy, any contemplation of law was considered a branch of ethics or moral philosophy as it should be.) They even have been arguing over whether their theories of law are descriptive, interpretative, normative, hermeneutical, descriptive/interpretative (whatever that means), and so forth apparently for no other reason than to listen to themselves talk. Again, as I stated before, since none of these meanings are predictive as a scientific wordgame would be, the intelligentsia can make up as many meanings as they want to fit into whatever wordgames they make up. In the end, it does not matter and no ones should care except for tenure committees.

Supposedly, they all want to make a "science of law" in which its wordgame is a social construct that possesses certain attributes by its very nature or essence as law whenever and wherever it happens. They disagree as to whether or not the essence of this social construct "law" includes morality. If it does not, according to Legal Positivism it only has legal obligations, rights, and duties created by a social process involving Rules of Recognition, Rules of Change, and Rules of Adjudication that by a Separability Thesis are separate from moral obligations but that allows lawgivers to consider other nonlegal "obligations" that according to Leiter cannot be "understood as *moral* obligations".[21] If it does not include morality, then law is law regardless of whether it is democratic, fascist, or whatever. For those philosophers of law who argue law must consider moral obligations, what morality would that be? Unclear, except they all agree it is not any type of religious morality; usually they mean the morality as decided by Oxford, Harvard, or Yale academia. How are nonlegal obligations different from moral obligations? (They are not, it is simply different words with the same meaning.) How does one make a "science of law" if the law is not a predictive wordgame concerned only with pragmatic truth that can be tested and falsified? (You cannot.)

I do not know and do not care about these academic questions and their academic answers because none of these issues with "law" as a universal are relevant to my question nor should they matter to any working class person nor anyone in any but the highest of social classes or their intelligentsia. The only descriptive universal attribute or value of the bound variable "law" is the one it possesses by its very nature and essence as a social construct whenever and wherever it happens: its special monopoly on violence to enforce itself. The realities of any law be it contract, tort, probate, estate, civil, criminal, tax, inheritance, administrative, and whatever, the unique and omnipresent feature of all law is that eventually even in the absence of any other obligation or in opposition to other obligations such as religion and matters of conscience, the law will violently enforce obedience as a matter of normative right.

The Legal Positivist H.L.A. Hart however was correct that this monopoly on violence as an attribute of law is not the same as a gunman's threat. It is in reality the same as a social group of gunmen's or a mob of gunmen's threats because law is a social construct; there is no such thing as private law. Though these days I should phrase it as a mob of gunpersons since women are now made-men in the mob that is law. If a criminal mob takes over an island and begins to enforce its oaths, code of conduct, contract rules, pragmatic obligations of care, rules of inheritance, family rules of care, and rules for maintenance and distribution of wealth on the island, with a little time and with the help of philosophers of law such as Leiter, it eventually becomes the government of Mob Island with its mob rules becoming its criminal law, contract law, tort law, estate law, probate law, and so forth. One of the purposes in life for

---

[21] Brian Leiter. *The Role of Judges in Democracies: A Realistic View.* pp. 2-3 and *generally.*

philosophers of law is to assist a mob of gunpersons in transforming themselves from a mob to being law; they essentially act as the mob's *consigliere*.

Philosophers of law ignore this necessary value or attribute in their philosophizing most likely unintentionally so as not to demean the meaning of their lives and because with few exceptions most have never actually practiced law so they do not know what they are describing nor how its different aspects work with each other; in fact, they consider practice as something beneath them, as something with which it is not worth getting their hands dirty. As trial attorneys describe appellate judges, they like to watch from on high the legal battle fought below, and when the dust and smoke of the battle clear they come down out of the hills and shoot the wounded.

Just as the meaning of science for philosophers of law everywhere has the same meaning, it is the intent of naturalized law everywhere to be the same wordgame wherever and whenever it is found: United States, Stalinist Russia, Great Britain, North Korea, wherever. According to naturalized law, law is law; it is has nothing to do with moral obligations because even if it did, they do not really exist in any sense other than the lawgiver's personal beliefs, opinions, "tastes", bias, and so forth — their morality, deceptively called nonlegal obligations to hide the same meaning of the words and the is-ought transition.

The only limit on these nonlegal obligations and the law's monopoly on violence is the physical reality of execution: how far will the law's enforcers or hitmen go before the one with the gun pointed at their head becomes suicidal.

As I stated up-front, I dislike and disapprove of this descriptive reality granting law a normative monopoly on violence and believe it ought not to be. Based on historical evidence and life experience, power corrupts; the unchecked power of law "ought" not to be in order to maintain a free and open society. There ought to be something to counterbalance it other than an opposing mob who wants its own monopoly on violence. America can now claim to be the oldest continuing modern democracy or republic — depending on how you define those terms. However, it is not the first of either; democracies and republics have come and gone before and were a well-known form of governance even in the ancient world among tribes and then on to city states. So much so that the philosopher Plato whom Leiter loves to criticize became history's first known sociologist by studying their rise and fall then developing a descriptive and interpretive theory allowing for predictions that have yet to be falsified by time. According to Plato, all states begin with kingship then evolve into timocracy or plutocracy; then oligarchy; then democracy; then anarchy; finally tyranny.[22]

George Orwell in *1984* accurately and succinctly described the new school tyranny that is presently the law and destined to be our future under the law:

> As compared with their opposite numbers in past ages, the new aristocracy is less avaricious, less tempted by luxury, hungrier for pure power, and, above all, more conscious of what they were doing and more intent on crushing opposition. This last difference was cardinal. By comparison with that existing today, all the tyrannies of the past were half-hearted and inefficient. The ruling groups were always infected to some extent by liberal ideas, and were content to leave loose ends everywhere, to regard only the overt act, and to be uninterested in what their subjects were thinking. Even the Catholic Church of the Middle Ages was tolerant by modern standards. Part of the reason for this was that in the past no government had the power to keep its citizens under constant surveillance. The invention of print, however, made it easier to manipulate public opinion, and the film and the radio carried the process further. With the development of television and the personal computer, and the technical advances which made it possible to receive and transmit simultaneously on the same instrument, private life came to an end. Every citizen, or at least every citizen important enough to be worth watching, could be kept for twenty-four-hours a day under the eyes of the police and in the sound of official propaganda, with all other channels of information closed. The possibility of enforcing not only complete obedience to the will of the State, but complete uniformity of opinion on all subjects, now existed for the first time.

> Nothing the citizen does is indifferent or neutral. His or her friendships, hobbies, behavior towards his or her spouse or lover, facial expressions, gestures, characteristic movements, tones of voice, words muttered while asleep -- all are jealously scrutinized. Not only any actual misdemeanor, but any eccentricity, however small, any change of habits, any nervous mannerism that could possibly be the symptom of an inner struggle, is certain to be detected. Endless purges, arrests, tortures, imprisonments, and disappearances are inflicted both as punishments for crimes which have been actually committed and as the systematic wiping-out of any persons who might perhaps commit a crime at some time in the future.

> And so today the determining factor in perpetuating a totally obsolete hierarchical society is the mental attitude of the ruling class itself. The problem, that is to say,

---

[22] Plato. *Republic, Book VIII.*

is educational. It is a problem of continuously molding the consciousness both of the directing group and of the larger executive group that lies immediately below it. Skepticism and hesitancy among the ranks of the rulers must be prevented. (As will be seen in Chapter 3, the best method of molding consciousness is continuous warfare.)

The consciousness of the masses (the "proles"), by contrast, needs only be influenced in a negative way. The masses could only become dangerous if the advance of industrial technique made it necessary to educate them more highly: but, since military and commercial rivalries are no longer of primary importance, the level of popular education is actually declining. What opinions the masses hold, or do not hold, is looked upon as a matter of indifference. They can be granted intellectual liberty because it is thought that they have no intellect. In a member of the ruling elite, on the other hand, not even the smallest deviation of opinion on the most unimportant subject can be tolerated.

All the beliefs, habits, tastes, emotions, mental attitudes that characterize our time are really designed to sustain the mystique of the rulers and prevent the true nature of present-day society from being perceived. A member of the elite is required to have not only the right opinions, but the right instincts. Many of the beliefs and attitudes demanded of him or her are never plainly stated, and could not be stated without laying bare the contradiction at the heart of modern-day hierarchical society. To maintain this regime, a continuous alteration of the past is necessary. Both the elites and the masses will tolerate present-day conditions because they have no standards of comparison. Everyone must be cut off from the past, as well as from other countries, because it is necessary for one and all to believe that everyone is better off than his or her ancestors and that the average level of material comfort is rising. But by far the most important reason for the constant readjustment of the past is to safeguard the validity of the system itself. It is not merely that speeches, statistics, and records of every kind can and must be constantly brought up to date in order to show that the fundamental principles of society are sound. No change in these basic principles -- work, commodity production, private property, the State -- can ever be admitted. For to change one's mind is a confession of weakness, and weakness cannot be tolerated in a "perfect" system.

...

From the point of view of our present rulers, therefore, the only genuine dangers are the splitting-off of a new group of able, under-employed, power-hungry people, and the growth of liberalism and scepticism in their own ranks. The problem, that is to say, is educational. It is a problem of continuously molding the consciousness both of the directing group and of the larger executive group that lies immediately below it. The consciousness of the masses needs only to be influenced in a negative way.

In principle, membership [in the Party] is not hereditary. The child of Inner Party parents is in theory not born into the Inner Party. ... . Nor is there any racial discrimination, or any marked domination of one province by another. Jews, Negroes, South Americans of pure Indian blood are to be found in the highest ranks of the Party, and the administrators of any area are always drawn from the inhabitants of that area. ... Its rulers are not held together by blood-ties but by adherence to a common doctrine. It is true that our society is stratified, and very rigidly stratified, on what at first sight appear to be hereditary lines. There is far less to-and-fro movement between the different groups than happened under capitalism or even in the pre-industrial age. Between the two branches of the Party there is a certain amount of interchange, but only so much as will ensure that weaklings are excluded from the Inner Party and that ambitious members of the Outer Party are made harmless by allowing them to rise. Proletarians, in practice, are not allowed to graduate into the Party. The most gifted among them, who might possibly become nuclei of discontent, are simply marked down by the Thought Police and eliminated. But this state of affairs is not necessarily permanent, nor is it a matter of principle. The Party is not a class in the old sense of the word. It does not aim at transmitting power to its own children, as such; and if there were no other way of keeping the ablest people at the top, it would be perfectly prepared to recruit an entire new generation from the ranks of the proletariat. In the crucial years, the fact that the Party was not a hereditary body did a great deal to neutralize opposition. The older kind of Socialist, who had been trained to fight against something called 'class privilege' assumed that what is not hereditary cannot be permanent. He did not see that the continuity of an oligarchy need not be physical, nor did he pause to reflect that hereditary aristocracies have always been short-lived, whereas adoptive organizations such as the Catholic Church have sometimes lasted for hundreds or thousands of years. The essence of oligarchical rule is not father-to-son inheritance, but the persistence of a certain world-view and a certain way of life, imposed by the dead upon the living. A ruling group is a ruling group so long as it can nominate its successors. The Party is not concerned with perpetuating its blood but with perpetuating itself. Who wields power is not important, provided that the hierarchical structure remains always the same. *1984*, George Orwell.

Given law's monopoly on violence that makes it essentially a new school Technological Society form of tyranny consisting of a few wearing judicial robes instead of one or a few wearing a military uniform, why tolerate law?

2. *What are the usefulness and use of the word "religion"?*

Unlike Leiter, I am not going to make up words describing religion while pretending my description is independent from my normative and pragmatic concerns. One can use the made-up words Rules of Recognition, Rules of Change, and Rules of Adjudication used by philosophers of law describing the communal social construct "law" just as easily to describe the communal social construct "religion" except for the Separability Thesis that would be changed to requiring religion to be distinct from law and legal obligations but allowing it to consider moral and "non-moral" obligations. For purposes of my question, I only care about religion as a social construct possessing by its very nature and essence as a social construct whenever and wherever it happens: 1) a belief in a morality of how a community ought to be distinct from the obligations of law; 2) recognizing the distinction "give to Caesar what belongs to Caesar, and give to God what belongs to God". For something to be a religion, it must have these attributes. Anything else is either a political movement or a matter/liberty of conscience.

Leiter completely ignores these two religious attributes that separate religion from morality and matters and liberty of conscience: religion is communal, a social construct just as law is communal and a social construct.

Obviously, my definition excludes many social constructs that are commonly considered religion and may include some that are commonly not considered religion, but this is my intention. An Eastern religion such as Islam requiring the state and religion to be one or an ancient religion of state worship such as Roman or Greek worship of the *polis* or Aztec unity of state and religion is useless to my normative goal of evenly counterbalancing law's monopoly on violence. They would simply be the new mob in town.

Existentially, one can no more have a private religion than one can have a private law. One can have a morality and matters of conscience as to how one ought to live life but religion is a communal or social construct of how a community ought to live life or how an individual within the context of a community ought to live life. Once the communal "ought" is lost, religion existentially becomes just another morality or matter of personal "conscience" just as law would become just another rule. A purely private religion is not existentially a religion in the same way that a purely private law is not a law — such private concepts are meaningless words as would be a private language.

Further, at least in Western Civilization, religion has a unique descriptive attribute that makes it distinct from any political movement seeking a normative power to enforce its morality: it recognizes a separation of normative power between religious power and the state, "give to Caesar what belongs to Caesar, and give to God what belongs to God".

Religion, unlike matters of conscience and political movements, can be and once was in the Western World a powerful check on the power of law as a normative power — "in the world but not of the world".

Thus the usefulness of the word "religion" to my wordgame and question is its pragmatic usefulness to check the tyranny of law. At least Western religions such as Christianity begin with the belief and hope of a loving God and use Rules of Recognition, Rules of Change, and Rules of Adjudication to develop what they admit to be a "morality" of what society "ought" to do. Religion fails miserably sometimes in acting on its morality but law has done no better and usually much worse. Without Western law's assumption — again, some would say hijacking — of the "tastes" of Western religion's Sermon on the Mount and Beatitudes and the power struggle within itself and with secular law as to the pragmatic requirements of such "tastes", there would be no Rules of Recognition, Change, and Adjudication different from those used in Aztec, Islamic, or ancient states.

That Leiter is clueless about the essential nature of morality and the essential difference between morality, matters of conscience, and religion is evident from his statement: "no one needs a moral theory, after all, to know whether they are against racism or in favor of racial equality, against chattel slavery or in favor of human freedom, against cruelty or in favor of treating people in a dignified way, against human misery or in favor of human happiness".[23] Of course they do, that is what morality is. They do not need a religion — unless they want to apply their morality to the community — but by definition they need a morality to evaluate the meaningless indifference of the universe and then evaluatively and perspectively to conclude how it ought to be. Morality is simply a system through which a person determines right and wrong conduct. It may not be a rational morality that goes beyond the initial irrational belief or opinion foundation or premise necessary to build a rationally explicit morality but so what? Morality by its nature begins as irrational, not only as an existentialist protest (in the non-Nietzsche sense) against the meaningless of the universe but also in order to avoid

---

[23] *The Role of Judges in Democracies: A Realistic View.* p. 5.

an infinite chain of "ought" statements. One must start with an initial irrational belief, opinion, conclusion, or something to make meaningful normative statements. If one is amoral, one does not care about any of the issues in Leiter's statement, and one is free to enjoy and share in the clarity, beauty, and power of the indifference of the universe. Only if one has a morality are the words of the stated beliefs meaningful in a normative sense.

Where was Leiter's beloved Nietzsche when he made this absurd statement about not needing a moral theory for the issues stated? In any naturalized view of reality, words such equality, freedom, cruelty, dignified, misery, and happiness are empirically meaningless. No one is equal or free. The universe by its essential nature is cruel. There is no dignity in life — life is miserable and then we die. Only the empirically delusional are happy. We cannot eliminate chattel or wage slavery by saying that all humans are empirically equal. Not only is no one empirically equal by any empirical measure of equality but such issue should be irrelevant to the issue of one person owning another legally as chattel or as a wage slave. In theory, if humans are unequal in any naturalized sense — that is based on sense experience and empirical observations — the law could justify slavery as it did in all social constructs throughout history based on such sense. Slavery in any form "ought" to be illegal because it is immoral regardless of what is said or rationally concluded by Leiter's beloved naturalized "evidence and reasons [as] understood in other domains concerned with knowledge of the world ... ordinary standards of evidence and rational justification ... common-sense and in science".[24]

A bunch of individuals with "matters of conscience" opposing law's monopoly on power is always at least economic suicide and usually physical suicide. A political movement opposing law is simply a mob of gunpersons trying to be the new mob controlling the neighborhood. Is religion the only option?

3. *What is the meaning of my question's "toleration"?*

The word "toleration" has as many uses and therefore meanings as there are things to tolerate and people to tolerate them. Prison guards tolerate prisoners as long as the prisoners do what they are told; under such toleration, prison is a very peaceful and

---

[24] Brian Leiter. *Why Tolerate Religion.* p. 19.

orderly existence but not a free and open society. At present, I can honestly say that during my 4 ½ years of sea duty on three boats that the old school Navy tolerated more freedom of speech among its submariners and other sailors than anyone does in the legal profession or in law school academia or even in the civilian world among its attorneys, students, and civilians. Neither is now a free and open society for speech but at least the Navy is not supposed to be.

I do not mean nominal toleration as the law means of religion.

The law in its demand for toleration of law is at the other end: absolute toleration of law — follow orders, do not cause trouble, or else. It even has the audacity to call this type of toleration "diversity". There are no exceptions except those law creates. Using this meaning leads to a very straightforward and simple answer to my question. Why tolerate law in the sense of absolute toleration of its demands? There is no reason for such toleration other than fear. It is the same toleration due a mob of gunpersons. I must tolerate them until I can oppose them.

The meaning I seek for "toleration" in my question is normative and pragmatic, so its meaning is not as simple as that which the law requires of itself. To give "toleration" useful meaning as a normative word in relation to law and religion, I begin with a rejection of the law's demand for absolute toleration based on historical reasoning and evidence that power corrupts and absolute power corrupts absolutely. Once I do that, my question becomes one of asking: why I must I accept the law's absolute power of violence if it does not work for a free and open society and there are alternatives? In a way, this seems to be word-playing, just replacing "tolerate" with "accept" plus a phrase. Unfortunately, there seems to be no way around it. The added phrase sufficiently describes the normative and pragmatic basis of my concerns to differentiate "toleration" from its nominal and absolute meanings, and thus is useful for the question at hand.

IV.   WHY TOLERATE LAW?

In answering my question, since it is essentially normative and pragmatic, as I have admitted, I accept as a given that anything with a monopoly on violence to enforce itself upon me and my community does not work for establishing, maintaining, or fostering a free and open society. It has never worked in the past, thus there is no reason to believe it will in the future absence the law's categorical demand unhinged from reason and evidence that we so believe and have faith in its nonlegal obligations in the same way religion demands faith in its moral obligations. Such monopoly does not work to promote a free and open society in the present consisting of a Technological Society well on its way to achieving Orwellian *1984* reality. In our Orwellian present and future, however, the Room 101 of our O'Briens will not be a room with a rat cage but a sterile, pleasantly decorated, warm, friendly room with a surround sound of aesthetically pleasing legal verbiage convincing everyone slavery is freedom negating substantive diversity of thought and conscious and complex and empathetic comic and tragic thought. Meanwhile, outside our Room 101, the law will be busy denying the truth that $2 + 2 = 4$ using as justification law and economics.

Not that religion is any better if given its own monopoly on violence. The essence of the historical battle for separation between church and state in Western Civilization first comes to life with his Honor Judge Pontius Pilate (a hero of Nietzsche) condemning to death a man he knew to be innocent by asking *"quid et veritas"*? Christianity condemns the act as immoral or amoral conveniently ignoring it is Christianity's dogma that it was necessary. Both law and religion will kill the innocent if for them need be especially if unchecked by other power.

So, I am left with determining whether there are alternatives to such special monopoly on violence for law. Historically, the alternatives going back to antiquity — when the state and religion were one — consist of finding either an internal or external armed mob willing to take on the armed mob that is law. The external means war. The internal requires civil war based on a communal unity of purpose established by tribal, class, family, ethnic or race, religious, or some other form of social bonding or loyalty strong enough to take on the law or religion.

War is not much of an alternative and I will give the benefit of a doubt to law on this issue because I do not see any legal cultures out there having any less of a monopoly on violence than American law if they militarily conquered us. I include Islam in this as an external force. As a warrior religion founded for the specific purpose of military and commercial conquest not recognizing the separation between church and state, Islam is not a religion but a state relative to the normative and pragmatic answer I am seeking to my question.

As far as the internal alternatives remaining, civil revolt based on class loyalty is the only one that has worked successfully for any considerable period of time without consequences that were as bad or worse than the law it was fighting. An example is The

Conflict of the Orders or the Struggle of the Orders in the Roman Republic between Plebeians (commoners) and Patricians (aristocrats) in which the Plebeians sought political equality with the Patricians. It materially affected the Constitution of the Roman Republic and kept the Republic a viable free and open society relative to the ancient world for 400 years. However, the United States has always and still does deny the reality of social classes, and it is too late now to accept such reality. In our modern Technological Society, even if individuals were to acknowledge social class allegiance it is no longer possible to do anything about it as the law would technologically quickly notice it and put a stop to it by violence as it has done to the other listed social loyalties and bonds.

As to the other listed social bonds and loyalties, it was not enough for the law simply to abrogate the laws that converted them into violent "ism's" such as racism. Acting as a monopoly should act, the law through law with the aid of modern technology has by law abrogated those social bonds and loyalties themselves to assure a sterile world lacking in any social bonds or loyalties outside of the law and thus assuring its racism and its other -ism's to be part of its monopoly. It even has the audacity to call cultural stagnation "multi-cultural" and its lack of substantive diversity "diversity".

In prior historical periods of social struggle against the violence of law, individuals always had at least one alternative other than the law for social and moral support such as these listed loyalties or at least family support to fight the law's monopoly on violence. Except for those in United States upper social classes and their intelligentsia who need no family support but have plenty of it, even family support is fairly quickly becoming meaningless now that the majority of American workers have never been married; and given that for those workers who have children and try to support them, of these children at least 40% and rising will be raised most of their lives by single parents with neither extended nor nuclear family support.[25] It is fine and encouraged by the law since it intends to be a new school substitute for all old school concepts of marriage and family anyway by becoming our Big Brother who we will eventually learn to love — or else. It is only a matter of time before the majority of workers are single and childless and children are either a luxury for the few that can afford them or a necessity manufactured under government regulation as needed by the

---

[25]

http://www.pewsocialtrends.org/2014/09/24/record-share-of-americans-have-never-married/;
http://www3.uakron.edu/schulze/401/readings/singleparfam.htm

law's Brave New World. New school racism and wage slavery of individuals is the new norm beloved by law with the same social and political effects as old school racism and chattel slavery only this type around it is not limited to any particular class.

Western religion for centuries has worked to control the law. Beginning with the Battle of the Milvian Bridge, on to Pope Leo saving Rome from sacking by Attila the Hun, on to the Battle of Vienna, and further, the power of Christianity has civilized Western law not the other way around. Though law school professors continually preach of the Magna Carta as the foundation of modern "rule of law" constitutional jurisprudence, they all seem to forget that it was Archbishop Stephen Langton of the Catholic Church who in 1215 incited and gathered the Barons together to create this document in an attempt to force even the King to admit submission to Divine Law. There would not have been a Renaissance or Enlightenment without the equal but separate struggle for power between church and state. Such examples are omnipresent throughout Western history. Whatever good is in Western law is there either because of Western religion or because of Western religion struggling with law as a counterbalance to their respective desires for a monopoly on violence.

These above descriptions are hinged to reason and evidence.

Unfortunately, religion has surrendered the battle. Though historians disagree, I view the paradigm shifting surrender as happening in the 20th Century World Wars as with so much else that shifted. Though the center to right Christian political parties in Germany kept the Nazi Party as a minority electoral party through successive elections despite the violence it used to intimidate voters, once they passed the Enabling Act of 1933 and legally took over as a tyranny, religion gave up the struggle and did as legally required — they tolerated law absolutely.

This surrender continued and has become complete in the last few decades. It is at the point now where millennia-old Christian communities in the Mideast have been eliminated through intentional and knowing genocidal application of Islamic law, yet the best Christianity can muster in defense is having its Pope stand at a balcony and waive the peace sign. "How many divisions does the Pope of Rome have?" — Josef Stalin. None, it no longer has any normative power having surrendered it to the law during the World Wars just as it surrendered its crusading powers centuries ago.

Leiter in the asking of the following question shows his pragmatic ignorance of what should be the most important attribute of religion by his critical comment finding "the devoutly religious among those who bomb abortion clinics".[26] From the Christian perspective, this criticism is the equivalent of complaining that we find "the devoutly religious among those who bombed legal human extermination camps in Germany", if they had done so which they did not. To any religion that believes regardless of whether it is by divine revelation or by rational beliefs, intuitions, or assumptions that life begins at conception and thus that abortion is infanticide and it "ought" not to be legal, such beliefs morally justify bombing legal abortion clinics in the same way such beliefs would morally justify bombing legal extermination camps to prevent the killing of six million adults. The fact that religions with such beliefs did not do so when extermination camps were legal is an argument for denying special toleration to both religion and law and not just one or the other. The fact that modern Western religion, despite the fact that they believe abortion is infanticide, is not bombing abortion clinics because they are legal in the same way that they did not call for a crusade to bomb German extermination camps because they were legal is undisputed evidence that it has surrendered to law.

Since the World Wars, it has been all down hill for Western religion acting as a counterbalance to law's monopoly on violence. Western religious have become more like Nietzsche than our intelligentsia who love him. The religious just want to meet once a week, hold hands, sing *Kumbaya*, hug the Turin horse and cry, and then go back to the real world of following orders, doing as told, and not making trouble for the law. From abortion to equal legal rights for corporations, to gay marriage, to secular control of religious education, to forced association by the religious with immoral acts, to meaningless toleration, and on to any legal battle one can name between law and religion, religion has lost — all the while law pontificating that it gives religion nonexistent special toleration. Not only has religion lost, but it lost its battles timidly and cowardly without a serious fight. It is a meaningless, worthless opponent to the monopoly of violence held by the law.

A.   The Answer to the Question of Why Tolerate Law

---

[26] *Why Tolerate Religion*, p. 19.

The law makes a categorical demand unhinged from reason and evidence that by necessity it must have a special monopoly on violence. By Leiter's definition, it is a religion and therefore by his own argument it ought not have this special toleration.

As far as my contemplation goes, if Western religion were the law's equal opponent in power, my answer would be: only tolerate the law's special monopoly on violence if it tolerates a separate by equal non-violent force of normative religion to counterbalance it, otherwise there is no normative or pragmatic reason to tolerate it. Law is just another mob to be feared and given only the usual toleration given any mob of gunpersons until we can find a better option. Unfortunately, modern Technological Society does not at present allow for any other option, so we are stuck. Political opposition would simply be another mob. Individual opposition through matters or liberty of conscience is ineffective as a surrender to the mob's protection or as economic or physical suicide.

Since Western religion has surrendered the battle, we have no choice but to tolerate law so that it does not kill us while we look for and hopefully find an equal opponent. I submit the opponent must be a naturalized version of existentialism and even nihilism if need. Just as scientific thought when necessary begins with anarchy, we may have to begin developing a counterbalancing force with nihilism. We must develop a naturalized existential philosophy of law founded upon a courageous human existentialism not a cowardly one founded on the aesthetics worship of Nietzsche that can only lead to a Hegelian world view destroying individual freedom and free and open societies.

V.   THE PHILOSOPHY BEHIND PHILOSOPHY OF LAW

Given that all normative statements including religious morality and the disguised morality of the law it calls non-moral obligations must begin with essentially irrational beliefs, opinions, or conclusions, what is the philosophy behind Leiter's normative conclusion that the law ought not give religion special toleration? According to Leiter's *The Truth is Terrible*, it is the philosophy of Frederick Nietzsche. This means there is no God; if there is, He is dead. "[A]ll of us are destined for oblivion". In contrast to the 89%

of American *hoi polloi* who believe in God,[27] Leiter has been "cleansed of theological superstitions" and the "fake immortality" of a nonexistent spiritual union with those that have struggled before us and that hopefully will struggle in the future against the indifference and outright hatred of us by the universe. Oohs! Should not have mentioned hope. Hope is an illusion; all is meaningless suffering. The only reason to prefer life to nonexistence in answer to "Schopenhauer's challenge" is the aesthetic creations of "the spectacle of genius, a spectacle incompatible with the triumph of ascetic moralities over the past two thousand years".[28] I assume Leiter and his work are one of these aesthetic creations of genius that give life meaning.

In *The Truth is Terrible*, Leiter praises the "Dionysian" perspective on life as life affirming compared to the life threatening perspectives of Plato, Socrates, the "crucified", and the Stoics. He seems to miss entirely the irony that Dionysus was a god while the others — including the "crucified" — were all human. This is not nihilism, nor was Nietzsche a nihilist. It is a cowardly attempt to defeat nihilism no better than the cowardice of modern Western religion.

Nietzsche? Really? Schopenhauer's challenge? In an age of science, with a whole universe waiting out there for us to discover, explore, and conquer, this is the best modern intelligentsia can come up with as a foundation for the normative "non-moral" obligations of its philosophy of law? That Western religion has trouble being equal in power to this nonsense further shows how low it has gotten.

I know Leiter is serious and expects to be treated seriously, but the image of academic dons in their bow tie suits after having led risk-adverse sheltered lives in which their only motivation and concerns were for success in their professional career; who now lead a sheltered exclusion from reality consisting of life-tenure positions in academia; standing at a classroom podium shaking their fist (metaphorically only of course, never physically) at heaven; and crying God is dead is a comical image at best and usually a very farcical image. They have not killed God, they have simply replaced Him with self-worship of themselves as demigods — just as the patrician Schopenhauer did of himself and his patrician class. Every time I imagine this image or read academic pontificating on Nietzsche, I can hear the song *"Wanna be a Gangsta"* by the band Body Count.

---

[27] Note 9, *supra*.

[28] Brian Leiter. *The Truth is Terrible*.

The story of Nietzsche and the Turin horse and the movie *Turin Horse* by Bela Tarr based upon that story say much about the dangerous hypocrisy of Nietzsche and the cowardly followers of his brand of existentialism and any philosophy of law they create. Their image of the suffering artist crying about suffering horses then going back to his apartment safe-place luxuries to have his mother take care of his delicate sensibilities while the *de facto* slave human owners of the Turin horse and the horse itself go back to work epitomizes the Technological Society intelligentsia view of reality. This concept that aesthetics and the genius of art are the only possible source of meaning in a meaningless universe explains why the intelligentsia creates so much beautiful verbiage that says nothing; after all, there is nothing more atheistically pleasing to reason then listening to itself talk or reading its words even if they do not say anything. However, if such philosophy is truly the *Terrible Truth* of the law as Leiter claims, it only serves as a further reason not to tolerate law *qua* law; not only because it is a mob of gunmen but it is a mob with certain tastes in art it wants to force me to buy with my taxes.

The tragic terrible truth is that this comical philosophy is a real source of meaning and brute normative force through law among our Outer and Inner Parties. It gives their lives meaning and a need to create a world in their image by a monopoly of force. Their aesthetic meaning goes on to admit treason to the existentialist struggle by raising Hegel to praise judges such as Richard Posner as a Hegelian "'Owl of Minerva', who has captured the moral ethos of his time and place".[29] Again, Leiter seems oblivious to the fact that Hegel's initial World Spirit and Owl of Minerva were the glory of the Prussian military state and the absolute rule of its Frederick William III.[30] Thus, though pretending to have an existential faith to the freedom of a Nietzsche, it is really to the tyranny of Hegelian state worship that is the foundation for modern law's nonlegal obligation demanding an unchecked monopoly on violence to enforce the law's World Spirit morality.

As if it were not bad enough that the law hides its morality as nonlegal obligations, it also wants to hide it as "economics". With the likes of judges such as Leiter's beloved Posner, it now also uses the word "economics" to hide its morality and its is-ought transition. The present fad of law-and-economics allows life-tenured judges in the secret of their chambers to arbitrarily decide what is the best economic goal for

---

[29] Brian Leiter, *In Praise of Realism (And Against 'Nonsense' Jurisprudence)* p. 24.

[30] *See generally.* Karl Popper. "The Open Society and Its Enemies".

society; then in court spend a few minutes and a few pages of briefs pretending to let lawyers and their clients, for whom they hold nothing but contempt, argue law; and then back in the secrecy of their chambers fabricate law and facts without any input from actual economists to achieve their arbitrarily chosen result. All the while, as would the Wizard of Oz, they tell the *hoi polloi* "pay no attention to the man behind the screen". Such terrible truth is not only reality for sophisticated con artists such as Posner, but even of the simplest and unsophisticated of con artists of the Inner Party. Present Supreme Judge Sonia Sotomayor stated in an Associated Press interview that she wanted to be a judge by age ten after watching a Perry Mason episode at which point she "realized that the judge was the most important player in that room".[31] If anyone is reading this, ask what were you dreaming about at age 10? At age 10, I was just trying to survive until the next day. If I did dream, it was about having love and a happy family; about the girl sitting next to me in class; to become an astronaut; an explorer of the world and the universe; to cure cancer; to become a military hero; or doing something great to help my fellow humans. The few times I watched Perry Mason, I sympathized with the innocent defendant being railroaded through the system by the powers — including the moron judge — miraculously saved from imprisonment or worse only by the hero Perry Mason. Supreme Sotomayor despite having a loving extended family supporting her path not only to survive but to prosper in life instead was dreaming of being the judge simply because the judge has the most power in the room. At age ten, she wanted to sit in judgment of fellow humans and jail them, ruin their families, ruin them financially, or do whatever else is necessary to have the powerful stay in power. This is the will to power mentality that demands absolute toleration to its monopoly on violence.

For the United States, inevitably falling into anarchy and eventual tyranny may be unavoidable if the law is our only technique to avoid such transition. The law has never in history stopped such a transition and often is the instrument for its occurring. As legal "enabling acts" start and continue, we cannot expect a legal culture willing to give a handful of judges a monopoly on violence to enforce their personal morality upon all of society simply because they wear judicial robes and call their morality nonlegal obligations and economics to stop tyrants wearing military or lab uniforms from doing

---

[31] http://www.today.com/id/30940443/ns/today-today_news/t/sotomayor-wanted-be-judge-age/#.WOasLWe1uyo

the same. Such a categorical expectation is unhinged from reason and evidence and is religion as Leiter defines it.

VI.   THE HOPE OF AN EXISTENTIALIST PHILOSOPHY OF LAW

Western Religion having surrendered the struggle, our one hope for an equal but separate normative power to counterbalance the soul crushing and mind numbing monopoly on power the law demands is not a godly Dionysian existentialism but a human and naturalized existentialism and the religious passion that a human communal normative existentialism would create. There is an entire universe out there waiting to be discovered, explored, and conquered. If the law has its way, as it has done throughout history, instead of acting to discover, explore, and conquer it, we will all be slaves to the small minority that are its Outer and Inner Party wasting precious time and resources on stupid arguments over whether Rule of Recognition, Rules of Change, and Rules of Adjudication are descriptive or interpretative; what pronouns to use; what gender is; and whether nonlegal obligations are different from moral obligations. Forget Nietzsche and our present religious and all sycophants and cowards that make categorical demands unhinged from reason and evidence for unchecked monopolies on violence. If God is to be found, He is out there somewhere because He is definitely not here. Let us all go look for him together. Let sycophants such as Leiter stay in their room or whatever safe place they have for hugging, whining, and admiring their self-centered aesthetic arbitrary verbiage regardless of whether they call it economics or nonlegal obligations.

Recognize that we cannot fight the universe and any tyranny of law individually, such is a suicidal struggle regardless of how well intentioned may be our individual liberty or "matters of conscience". Politics is simply an opposing mob of gunpersons. We can oppose a social construct with a monopoly on violence such as law only by an equal but separate social construct normative power whose essence is nonviolent. The struggle of life requires a communal act of hope and a normative belief of what ought to be including a morality of nonviolence: a religion. As it has done throughout history, the law rather than have a free and open society would rather see much of humanity stuck in slavery in order to maintain a status quo of law and order — only this time around it is wage slavery instead of chattel slavery. In order to defeat the inevitable violent tyranny of the law's demand for absolute toleration of it, with religion gone, it appears we must first embrace nihilism not avoid it. Communal creations of normative power are not created by agreement and peace, just as with scientific progress they are created by disagreement and struggle. In the absence of disagreement and struggle as equal but separate powers between law and old school religion, the only option is first to use nihilism to create disagreement and struggle. From this forge of struggle between law and naturalized human existentialism, hopefully new school religion will rise to take on law as an equal but separate power to create a free and open society.

To bring existential religion back to life or to give it life, we most certainly should not join in condemnation of the dead universally done by our Outer and Inner Parties through the likes of Leiter on the right equaled by the likes of a Ta-Nehisi Coates on the left — neither of which are the great minds and genius the intelligentsia worships them as. Instead, maintain your humanity and do not replace God with yourself as demigod. We should join both our Honored Dead and dishonored dead in a leap-of-faith struggle by continuing the struggle. The struggle is not "between the world and me", it is between the world and us:

> Take up our quarrel with the foe
> To you, from failing hands, we throw
> The torch: be yours to hold it high
> — *In Flanders Fields* by John McCrae

In this conclusion to my essay, I am only trying to lay a foundation for further contemplation and development of a naturalized existential philosophy of law. I hope to develop further details at a later date. Is there a universal thing called "law"; are there not just particular laws? How about religion? Is there a universal thing called "religion"; are there not just particular religions? I want to leave emphasizing that such development need not reject analytic philosophy, being naturalized with scientific thought, nor the philosophy of language as is done by so many continental especially nihilist philosophers. Existentialism begins with three basic analytical premises commonly shortened to the colloquialism of "existence precedes essence". In this colloquialism, there are three analytical premises that reverse the successful portion of Cartesian criticism of skepticism: "I am"; "I am therefore I think"; "I am and I will". Accepting these three premises as true existentially gives the rational mind the minimum of three variables it needs to create logic and use it to fight against the universe and its will to kill us and our community and for humanity to engage in the struggle that is life: $x, x \rightarrow y, x \wedge z$. Binding these variables by values is the beginning of all the complexities of logical thought.

The problem faced by existentialism is talking about the existential truth of the initial three premises. This seems to be a situation of "whereof one cannot speak, thereof one must be silent". However, this warning only applies to logical thought. One can still talk about the reality of these three premises illogically in the same way that one begins normative speech by beginning with irrational premises: by such language techniques as analogy, fiction, dialectical reasoning, (reasoning that rejects the classical law of non-contradiction), emotion, and anything else that works to get a meaning across.

The power of scientific language is its firm anchoring to both ends of fact and theory successfully using the past to predict the future. Existentialism is firmly anchored in fact; the problem is theory. As with any language or wordgame, the details of this firm anchoring are much disputed among philosophers of science. The line between non-science, pseudo-science, and science is difficult to establish and they often overlap. Luckily, again, philosophy of law is as sophomoric about philosophy of science as it is about language and thus avoids most of these disputes. However, there are three agreed upon universal attributes of scientific wordgames that make scientific language unique that existentialism must remember and understand for creation, attraction, and development of a philosophy of law: the use of Ockham's Razor at least as a heuristic technique if not an ontological one; its goal of using the past to predict the future; and thus by its falsifiability when its predictions fail.

In addition, regardless of one's morality, for studying philosophy of law, one must accept that none of these scientific attributes apply to the other end of the language wordgame spectrum consisting of morality: Ockham's Razor is useless for any purpose other than marketing — *i.e.*, "thou shall not kill" is good marketing but the books of exceptions are the real substance; it seeks not what is but what ought to be either now, in the future, or in both; and thus can only be falsified by assent — either by the individual or community whose morality it is. Regardless of whether this existential reality is good or evil, the existential reality is that scientific wordgames are rational processes that may have an irrational foundation in existential creativity or imagination but morality is an irrational process from start to finish that avoids being an infinite chain of "ought" statements only by starting either with Divine revelation or by individual or communal will to power beliefs, feelings, intuitions, or hopes.

The admission of irrationality as a foundation and substantive force is the keystone to making existentialism a force equal to religion for counterbalancing the tyranny of law. It must not in anyway condemn nor ignore the factual reality of history. It is what it is. "The slave begins by demanding justice and ends by demanding a crown". — Albert Camus. It is an existential fact of reality.

These analytic and existential considerations at this point are contingent upon what we used to call in the military: a will to fight. Have *hoi polloi* given on up continuing the struggle as have religion and intelligentsia? If so, we are not only destined to live in a Technological Society in which war is peace, freedom is slavery, ignorance is strength, stagnation is multi-cultural, and sameness is diversity, but, more significantly, we will lack the meaning in life and sense of community created by fighting and struggling against it. I love to paraphrase George Patton's comment on a future of technological wonder weapons that will soon, if not already, be applicable to law: "My God, I do not see the wonder in them. Killing without heroics. Nothing is glorified, nothing is reaffirmed. No heroes, no cowards. No humanity, no emotion, and no soul involved. Only those that are left alive and those that are left dead."

I end not with the Dionysian cowardice of a Nietzsche or Schopenhauer. I end first with an existential prediction of what will happen if the special toleration giving the law a monopoly on violence is not removed. I then leave with words of courage involving existential humans from the crucified to Camus with whom we can create a social construct religion as a separate but equal nonviolent normative power to counterbalance the present and inevitable tyranny of law and its violence — thus provide the only pragmatic justification for tolerating law:

> Power is not a means; it is an end. One does not establish a dictatorship in order to safeguard a revolution; one makes the revolution in order to establish the dictatorship. The object of persecution is persecution. The object of torture is torture. The object of power is power. — George Orwell, *1984*.

> It requires courage not to surrender oneself to the ingenious or compassionate counsels of despair that would induce a man to eliminate himself from the ranks of the living; but it does not follow from this that every huckster who is fattened and nourished in self-confidence has more courage than the man who yielded to despair. — Soren Kierkegaard.

I leave Sisyphus at the foot of the mountain! One always finds one's burden again. But Sisyphus teaches the higher fidelity that negates the gods and raises rocks. He too concludes that all is well. This universe henceforth without a master seems to him neither sterile nor futile. Each atom of that stone, each mineral flake of that night filled mountain, in itself forms a world. The struggle itself toward the heights is enough to fill a man's heart. One must imagine Sisyphus happy.

— Albert Camus, *The Myth of Sisyphus.*

References

A TRIAL ATTORNEY'S PERSPECTIVE: TWO DOGMAS OF LAW SCHOOL ACADEMICS

TABLE OF CONTENTS

FROM A TRIAL ATTORNEY'S PERSPECTIVE: TWO DOGMAS OF LAW SCHOOL ACADEMICS AND THEIR EFFECT UPON THE FUTURE OF LAWYERING

Valeriano Diviacchi

J.D. - Harvard Law School

I.   PROLOGUE

Modern law school academics in the United States are dominated by two major schools of thought: law and economics; critical theory. The most recent popular version of the latter calls itself critical realism. Both schools are conditioned upon two dogmas they claim must be recognized by jurisprudence and policy decisions in law. In critical theory, its foundational dogma states there exists a fundamental empirical distinction between situational influences and individual influences. This dogma exists in law and economics by a multiple of names, all making the same fundamental distinction but in disguised forms.   In the school of law and economics, situational influences are dogmatically defined as simply a set, sum, or collection of individual influences. Both schools of thought share another dogma: a belief that normative statements can be derived from empirical statements. Academics and their believers in both schools want to be anything, such as economists, psychologists, anthropologists, sociologists, physicists, and onward, anything but lawyers for whom they both exhibit nothing but contempt making me at least wonder why they went to law school in the first place though I suspect the answer is for the power. As a practicing attorney my whole career in law, I write this essay as a representative of a dying breed (perhaps justly so): trial work and the art of lawyering. Both dogmas and the contempt for the practice of law that goes with them are not only worthless to jurisprudence but the constant bickering over them and associated paper churning verbiage lacking substance pontificated by those who are the law's teachers serve only to destroy the credibility of jurisprudence and its usefulness for maintaining and passing on to posterity a free, prosperous, and open society. These dogmas and their contempt for the practice of law prevent progress in jurisprudence from catching up and paralleling scientific learning, an update it desperately needs if it will ever be anything more than the under-laborer for the few who are or want power over the many.

II. THE NATURE OF THE PROBLEM

As I will begin to analyze next in this essay, even in the simplest of problems in jurisprudence such as the proverbial "gun-to-the-head" case examples, the dogmas at issue do nothing useful but serve only to blind the search for the forest by concentrating on the trees. I will concentrate my analysis of the first dogma in the form it exists as a foundation for the new fad of critical realism because this analysis once understood will easily translate into an analysis of the equivalent dogma in law and economics that has had much more time to hide itself in the trees. For this purpose, I will reference examples of the dogma at work in the law review article entitled *"The Situation: An Introduction to the Situational Character, Critical Realism, Power Economics, and Deep Capture"* by Professors Jon Hanson and David G. Yosifon as this article seems to be the first gospel and foundation gospel for the bible of critical realism. I will refer to it as the Situation.

Though nominally hidden, the second dogma is substantively and essentially the same for both critical legalism and law and economics thus the analysis will not need to be split.

The Situation article begins with, contains within it, and ends with pages of warning and advice on how the readers need to open their minds, contest their most "reassuring self-perceptions", read "mindfully", and avoid being hypocrites who attach to other persons ignorance of truth while ignoring their own ignorance. After which, the authors of the Situation routinely, constantly, repeatedly, and to all indications unknowingly proceed to violate all of this warning and advice. I do not want to repeat their lecturing and risk becoming a hypocrite myself but it is important to have some sense and analysis of the hypocrisy involved to get an appreciation of the harmful, blinding effect these dogmas have upon jurisprudence and lawyering, in fact, upon basic reasoning skills and rational argument.

The nature of the problem of these blinding effects on both the substance, essence, and credibility of jurisprudence are most evident when the critical realism authors of the Situation try to be physicists instead of lawyers at pages 155 - 56 by using a "thought experiment" involving plane travel and then at multiple pages beginning at page 206 where they pontificate about the Catholic Church's initial rejection of the physics of Galileo as an example of "capture".

The plane travel "thought experiment" depicts an airplane passenger getting up from his seat, traveling to the bathroom, and returning fifteen minutes later. The authors than ask you to "estimate the distance that the old man traveled between leaving and returning to his seat." Now, if you are a reasonably prepared, reasonably educated trial attorney with some diversity in life experience, you would immediately note that this question at a minimum lacks a proper foundation, is misleading, misstates the facts, assumes facts not in evidence, and, even if these problems as to form are resolved, is a question that only would be relevant and have probative value for any reasonable inquiry into truth if asked of a qualified expert witness. However, the authors as law professors are not trying to be lawyers, they are trying to be physicists. As physicists, they answer, "If you are like most people ... you estimated thirty feet. A more accurate estimate, however, would be roughly 1000 times greater than that — approximately 150 miles. In other words, most people see the man moving within the plane, but miss his situation, the plane itself. ... Indeed, when one takes those additional situational forces [movement of the Earth, solar system, the galaxy, the universe] into account, the old man moved ... something closer to 350,000 miles." As a trial lawyer, my first instinctual response to this individual/situational distinction is, "how is a traveler walking on an airplane" any less "situational" than an "airplane flying on the earth"? I am getting ahead of myself. By admitting the question into the evidence considered in the <u>Situation</u>, the authors prove themselves unskilled trial lawyers; by allowing the answer in, they in addition prove themselves unskilled physicists even at an amateur or sophomoric level.

If my above lawyering objections were resolved and then only an expert witness physicist was allowed to answer the question, the first answer would probably be a question: "I cannot answer your question as posed, do you want me to use classical physics or modern relativity physics?" Since the <u>Situation</u> seems to love Galileo, to be consistent with that love, I answer "please use classical physics." At which point, the answer would probably be another question: "what inertial reference frame do you want me to use?" To keep things simple, I would answer "use the plane". To which the "truth" would be "approximately 30 feet". If I had answered, "use the earth"; the "truth" would be "approximately 150 miles." If we really wanted to challenge our "thought" instead of playing academic games, I should have answered his first question "please use modern relativity physics." To which, the physicist would have responded with another question, "what coordinate system do you want me to use and from what coordinate do you want me to measure?" In response, if I had answered "from the coordinate of the traveler with his point and coordinate remaining the same in any coordinate system", the "truth" would have been "zero distance traveled". What would have been the physicist's answer if I had asked the witness to use pure quantum physics without simplification for scale? Engage in a real thought experiment by finding this answer yourself, learn something, and thus do something the authors of the <u>Situation</u> for some reason could not be bothered or could not do.

If the plane travel "thought experiment" had been approached from a lawyering perspective, we would have had an actual thought and learning experience. Instead we got a differentiation between the "individual" situation of the traveler and the "situational" situation of the plane, earth, and so forth. A differentiation that no physicist would make because to science one inertial reference frame or coordinate system is as good as any other. Which one to use is relative to what they are trying to predict. So, again, "how is a traveler walking on an airplane" any less "situational" than an "airplane flying on the earth"? Is it simply because the authors of the <u>Situation</u> want it to be distinct in order to prove their argument that they are distinct? These questions are not considered in the "thought experiment", apparently it is assumed that this distinction is either self-evident or accepted based on their authority — that is, the distinction is dogma.

The enormity of the blindness to reality, despite calling itself critical realism, involved from such dogma is more evident in the <u>Situation</u>'s dealing with the Catholic Church's initial rejection of the physics of Galileo that goes on for pages of verbiage that says nothing.

So, how does the <u>Situation</u> cover Galileo? Do they act lawyerly and thus review, examine, and cross examine the best evidence: the hearing records, expert submissions, evidence, and documents of the inquisition of Galileo still available for review and much of it on the internet? Do they take evidence or testimony from historians, theologians, and physicists on the subject? No, apparently there is no need for that. After all, they are not just lawyers, they are historians, theologians, and physicists; so, they quote hearsay from other lawyers and tell us themselves what happened as self-evident truth. According to them, what happened is "capture." The Catholic Church was one of the mighty powers of the 17th Century. Galileo, while a student and then a professor teacher at two Catholic universities was a free-thinking lover of truth with a new "true" idea of the nature of our solar system but this "individual" influence on society was powerless against the "situational" influence of the Catholic Church whose power allowed it to distort and twist the academic and scholarly experts of the times to its irrational purely religious view of the solar system. As a result of this alleged capture, the authors tell us, an innocent individual was wrongly persecuted and silenced by Pope Paul V and a Cardinal Bellarmine denying society the "truth". According to the <u>Situation,</u> if not for this "capture" of the expert witnesses who testified and of the evidence presented at his inquisition, the experts would have supported Galileo and the truth would have been known earlier and without punishment of Galileo. According to the authors, this "answer is obvious".

Whoa, a powerful concept this "capture" based on this distinction between individual and situational influences. Again, as a lawyer, my initial instinct is to ask how are Galileo's teachings reached during years of study, examination, and teaching using the resources of two Catholic universities an example of "individual" influence whereas the Pope and Cardinal's teachings reached as a result of years of study, examination, and teaching using the resources at Catholic universities "situational"? There may be a difference of degree, but how are they different in kind? Does this distinction mean the Divinity School and the Philosophy Department at Harvard are "situational" influences whereas the Law School and Economics Department at Harvard are "individual" influences? Has anyone told the theologians and philosophers at Harvard about their situational power over law and economics that I suggest would be a surprise to them? Is individual influence the egg and situational influence the chicken? If so, which set of teachings is the egg and which the chicken? Which influence came first, the egg or the chicken?

Perhaps it is just a question of power? In his time, Galileo as an individual obviously had less power in every respect than the institution of the Catholic Church, but this would not be true of the individual Charles VII, the Emperor of the Holy Roman Empire, nor of the Pope. If it is an issue of the degree of power controlled, then we should call it an issue of the degree of power. Galileo had little individual power because of his situation as a student and teacher, Charles VII and Pope Paul V had large individual power because of their situations as emperor and pope. We can describe both sets of power honestly and truly either as "situational" or as "individual" depending on the speaker's intentions not upon any fundamental difference in the nature of "power" as that word is used in English neither in the circumstances of "capture" nor to the extent anyone advocates for its inclusion in jurisprudence. If "capture" means the Catholic Church was more powerful than Galileo, than should we just say so and get on with a Marxist analysis of law as simply a monopoly of violence and forget about the useless word "capture" based on the useless distinction between individual and situational influences whose use is dependent solely on the intent of the speakers not on the facts spoken about? The authors do not consider these questions. Again it is assumed the "answer is obvious" as either self-evident or based on their authority — that is, the distinction is dogma, the same as any dogma issued by the Catholic Church or any church.

Instead of being a historian, theologian, or physicist, let's try to be lawyerly and engage in the critical thought and examination of the alleged "capture" of Galileo's "truth" that would be required if it ever came up as an issue for trial. I should start by seeing what theologians say about it since it is a theological issue but I am practical enough to know that raising theology in an essay submission to the closed-minded culture of law school is a guarantee that it will be trashed. I actually hope and want someone to read this essay some day, so I will ignore theology.

What do historians tell us about the Galileo Inquisition? Historically, what happened is that Galileo while a student and then a professor at two Catholic universities developed a heliocentric theory of our solar system that he could not support at the time by any evidence because the necessary math and physics had not as yet been created and developed. The Church had a formal, open hearing on the matter in which Galileo was allowed to face and to respond to his accusers consisting of qualified, prominent, academic scientific authorities of the time who all disagreed with him and submitted argument and evidence to substantiate their disagreement. Based on such undisputed expert testimony and Galileo's inability to respond with anything other than unsubstantiated theory, the inquisitor Cardinal Bellarmine after review of his conclusions by the Pope personally ordered Galileo "... to abandon completely... the opinion that the sun stands still at the center of the world and the earth moves" as a physical truth. However, the Church did allow him to discuss such theory as a mathematical and philosophic idea. Thus, as the necessary mathematical and physical theories developed, eventually the heliocentric theory became widely accepted as scientific "truth" at Catholic and all universities. From a lawyering perspective, this was not a bad adjudicatory process overall nor result. Much better than anyone would now get before being terminated, removed, or arrested in our supposedly more open-minded society if one even tried to open a discussion at one's employment, in class, or in a public forum let along argue the politically incorrect stance on such topics as homosexuality, racism, sexism, or abortion.

How about the physics? It turns out that according to the modern general relativity physics of the last hundred years, the concept of an inertial reference frame that is necessary for either a heliocentric or geocentric model of the solar system does not exist. All we can do is establish coordinate systems for space-time in which the only requirement is that each point have a unique coordinate. So, according to modern physics, if we had a mind or computer sophisticated enough to deal with the enormous and convoluted mathematical complexities involved, we could choose and use a coordinate system with the revolving earth at the center and the sun revolving around it. Since real science accepts and practices Ockham's Razor as heuristic technique for its conceptual choices, real physics chooses the sun as the center of its coordinate system thus greatly simplifying the math and achieving a much more pragmatic model.

So, let's see what we have. A Cardinal Bellarmine condemning a person before him for ideas reached at one of the universities he supervises after a full evidentiary hearing and review that included expert witnesses to which the accused had a right to face and respond and to whom he did face and respond was persecution and "capture". So, what is it when two secular legal scholars as representatives of one of the most powerful legal cultures in history use solely their chosen written hearsay with no opposition submitted from anyone to condemn the dead and an entire millennia old religious culture? Is this like super-persecution and super-capture? If Cardinal Bellarmine was a tool for situational influences trying to avoid the absolute truth that the earth revolves around the sun, are the two secular legal scholars who wrote the <u>Situation</u> tools for situational influences trying to avoid the truth that there is no absolute truth about what revolves around what in space-time?

Is the absolute truth that if modern jurisprudence wants to approach reasoning in the same way as science, it should also accept Ockham's Razor as a heuristic technique and stop creating unnecessary dogma about distinctions and relationships such as "capture" simply to boast the egos of its academics and their worshipers who see in the law a means for power instead of controlling power but who do not want to call it power? It is with the hope that the answer to this last question is in the affirmative that I get into the body of this essay.

III.   FOUNDATION DOGMA OF CRITICAL REALISM

The words "situational influences" and "individual influences" (sometimes also called "individual dispositions") routinely appear as empirical distinctions in critical legalism essays without definition and without criteria for differentiating between the two. It is assumed that everyone knows what they mean and how to distinguish them. An assumption that is not very lawyerly because a proper foundation for argument and evidence is supposed to be the starting point for considering either. Also, as any collection of examples of these distinctions taken from critical legalism with show, these words are used inconsistently and randomly for different uses in different types of arguments varying from analogy and deduction to induction and rhetorical. Since in the modern world of language, the meaning of a word is supposedly its use, inconsistent and random use implies different meanings. For simplicity, since quantity of examples does not affect my analysis, I will primarily reference their uses in the Situation. In footnote 103 of that their article, "dispositionist" or "situationist" is defined as "attributional perception" while "dispositional" and "situational" are defined as the "attributional truth of the matter". The criteria of how "perception" becomes a "truth" are not stated but is dependent on whether they personally consider the causation for any given events to be either situational influences or individual influences. Thus, this footnote does not help with defining nor as criteria by which we can define the distinction.

Before I head into the convoluted uses of these words in academic critical legalism essays, I want to make logical and empirical sense of their standard uses.

Supposedly, the clearest and simplest exemplification of the fundamental distinction between "individual" and "situational" influences is having a gun pointed at my head, an example cited repeatedly in the Situation. In this situation, unless I am crazy, my individual options are completely controlled by the situation of having a gun pointed at my head. I agree that this situation is one of the simplest problems faced by jurisprudence in any area of law, be it contract, property, tort, criminal, or whatever. Simple and clear --- until you try to analyze it in terms of "individual" and "situational" influences. Having a gun pointed at me controls my options only if it is loaded. Undoubtedly, until proven otherwise, a person would assume the gun is loaded. So, what is controlling me, is it the situation of the gun pointed at me or the individual assumption that the gun is loaded? When having a gun pointed me, it may or may not be loaded, but a reasonable person will always assume it is loaded until proven otherwise. So, the actual dominant influence that is always present is not the situation of the gun pointed at me, but the individual influence of the assumption that it is loaded. Or is this reasonable person standard situational? But hold it, I always have that assumption because in our society of common gun ownership and use, it is common knowledge guns shoot projectiles that will blow my brains out. So, we are back to the dominant influence being the situational influence of having guns in society that blow brains out? But wait, the situational influence exists because individuals love having and using guns, it gives them individual joy; so we are back to an individual influence. This can go on for days. This is nonsense. If the individual/situational distinction uselessly and unnecessarily messes up one of the clearest and simplest problems faced by jurisprudence, how can it possibly help dealing with anything that has any subtlety or complexity? It can't.

The statement "I want to earn a big salary" seems to be an example of an individual influence. The statement "baseball players earn big salaries" seems to be an example of a situational influence. Nominally, purely from the point of semantics and syntax, the word "dispositional" is linguistic short hand for any statements expressing some form of "I want" and "situational" is linguistic shorthand for any statement expressing some form of "what is". This purely linguistic distinction in meaningless to critical realism unless the distinction is also teleological: the two words are supposed to represent two different or distinct types of causes for acts or events. For purposes of this essay, I will use the word "cause" to also include correlation as is done in all discussions involving the dispositional/situational distinction and therefore will ignore as irrelevant whether there is a difference between causation and correlation.

From the teleological perspective, purely as abstract concepts, the difference appears to be that dispositional means an internal attribution of causation while situational means an external attribution of causation. As abstractions, these distinctions get us into the same practical mess as the gun-pointed-at-head and the analytic mess that has plagued philosophers of language since antiquity: how do we differentiate between internal and external causes. Is there such a thing as an internal or private language? "I want to earn a big salary", why? Because big salaries buy one a lot of food, cars, houses, bikes, and planes; because it is a source of economic power; because the rich have a lot of money; so forth. If big salaries did not buy these things or power, no one would want money unless they were collectors of paper; even in that case, one would want to collect checks because they are paper and so many things are made of paper; have historical significance; are worth money; make people smile when they look at them; and so forth. The "want" of money are all correlated with external attributes. Is there an "intent" that exists in the individual that is different from the object and external manifestations of the "intent"? What does this "intent" look like, sound like, feel like, how do I measure it? If you cannot answer me because the experience of intent is purely private, how is it that you know the person "intends" anything and have a word for it? For the words "intent" or "internal" to have any meaning, they must have some sort of external verification and a set of criteria for correct application that must be accessible to others as well as to me: that is that are external.

In the abstract, this problem occurs with every attempt to speak about supposedly "internal" causes that are distinct from "external" causes. I do not see in critical theory any intent or any acts of wanting to jump into this philosophical mess. Though they want to be anything but lawyers, critical realists show no intend of wanting to be philosophers contemplating the nature of the universe. Critical realists want the power to act on the world and make the world in their image, which is why they became lawyers.

Their way out of it is by actually acting like lawyers for once. They do not deal in abstract concepts but always in every writing or argument that I have seen in critical theory tie the stated attribute to a relevant question. So, in response to the question, "why do you want to be a baseball player"; the answer "I want to earn a big salary" is an answer they claim of internal attributes and thus dispositional while an answer of "baseball players earn big salaries" is external and thus situational. Does this relationship of question to answers work to define the distinction they claim exists? It works in the sense of making the answers have meaning — or, as a lawyer would say, the answers are now relevant and probative. But, does the dispositional/situational distinction now make any sense? No, it makes no more sense than the internal/external cause distinction and has the same contradictions. Both answers substantively and essentially say the same thing and necessarily imply each other relevant to the question asked. The choice of how to express the answer is a nominal choice of grammar dependent on what the speaker is trying to prove changing nothing substantively or essentially for purposes of jurisprudence.

Maybe the problem is that I am dealing solely with an answer to a question to a person about himself or herself. Many times, the distinction in critical realism comes up when persons are answering questions about other persons thus bringing into the mix the "fundamental distribution error". (Since this is an essay on law, I am using persons also to refer to legal fictions such as corporations.) So, for example, I am in a car accident. My statement, "the other driver was a big, stupid, careless fellow" seems to be dispositional. The statement "mine and his car should have had anti-lock brakes" seems to be situational. Unless you take the politically incorrect position that the other driver

170

wanted to be a "big, stupid, careless fellow", how are the other driver's physical, intelligence, or educational limitations in anyway less situational to the accident than the other driver's lack of anti-lock brakes? The difference is one of degree not of kind. What if one does take the politically incorrect position that the other driver wanted to be a "big, stupid, careless fellow"? Again, as with internal, how do you know he wanted that? He failed to attend drivers' ed; he could have had his father drive him; he could have put anti-lock brakes on his car but did not; he could have gone slower; he left a suicide note; from the words he spoke; so forth. If you are going to use intent to try to create the dispositional influence, how are you going to eliminate it from the so-called situational influence? "My car should have had anti-lock brakes"; why didn't it? "I did not want to pay for it". "I liked the color of this car instead of the one with anti-lock". "I believe anti-locks are dangerous". "I did not know I could get anti-locks", and so forth. The difference in answers is dependent on what questions are asked not on any fundamental empirical difference in the teleological nature of the answers.

The information provided in these answers for jurisprudence and legal policy purposes — really for any purpose — is the same in both the dispositional and situational facts. The creation of this distinction for purposes of jurisprudence and policy decisions in law is worthless and adds no more information than the answers or any associated acts before adding the distinction. It is important for jurisprudence to make policy decisions on truth or at least upon a search for truth not on unnecessary distinctions that are of no aid in deciding the truth. For purposes of deciding and enforcing normative principles upon society as "law", a situation by necessity includes the acts and thoughts of the individuals stuck in it, and individuals by necessity physically and intellectually exist in situations. There is no way to fundamentally divide situation and individual as distinct causes.

As science has known and incorporated into scientific theory for more than fifty years, the language of theory and fact is a fabric of intertwined words, none of which have meaning on their own but only relative to the whole:

> The totality of our so-called knowledge or beliefs, from the most casual matters of geography and history to the profoundest laws of atomic physics or even of pure mathematics and logic, is a man-made fabric which impinges on experience only along the edges. Or, to change the figure, total science is like a field of force whose boundary conditions are experience. A conflict with experience at the periphery occasions readjustments in the interior of the field. Truth values have to be redistributed over some of our statements. Re-evaluation of some statements entails re-evaluation of others, because of their logical

interconnections -- the logical laws being in turn simply certain further statements of the system, certain further elements of the field. Having re-evaluated one statement we must re-evaluate some others, whether they be statements logically connected with the first or whether they be the statements of logical connections themselves. But the total field is so undetermined by its boundary conditions, experience, that there is much latitude of choice as to what statements to re-evaluate in the light of any single contrary experience. No particular experiences are linked with any particular statements in the interior of the field, except indirectly through considerations of equilibrium affecting the field as a whole. Two Dogmas of Empiricism, Willard Van Orman Quine.

(I will argue later — unfortunately for jurisprudence and its hope of becoming a science but fortunately for the hope of having a free, open, and prosperous society — the fabric of jurisprudence is normative language fabric forever separated from any empirical language fabric.)

It is an obvious truth that in language we use the words "individual" and "situation" in various forms and for various uses. In response to a question asking me what caused Caesar to die, I have an option of many true answers: "Brutus stabbed Caesar"; "Brutus the Roman politician stabbed Caesar to prevent him becoming a dictator"; "Brutus the Roman politician stabbed Caesar because of political and financial pressure from his family and other Senators"; "Cassius, Brutus, brothers Casca, and Minucius all stabbed Caesar in the Roman Senate to protect the Republic"; "multiple opposing senators in a conspiracy to protect their power in the Senate stabbed Caesar"; "Caesar let himself be caught in the Senate surrounded by his enemies"; "Caesar was caught by himself in the Senate by his enemies"; "he bled to death"; "one of the 35 stab wounds pierced his heart"; and hundreds if not thousands of other options. If I wanted to be allegorical, I could even truthfully answer, "It was Caesar's ambition that killed him." Some of these answers reference an individual instead of the individual's situation while some reference the situation instead of the individual and some both. Regardless of what so-called social scientists or even real scientists may do with the question of what caused Caesar's death, there is no basis and there is no method in jurisprudence to add to the complexity of the question "what killed Caesar" by fabricating a fundamental distinction in the answers between situational influences and individual influences. For purposes of deciding and enforcing normative principles upon society as law, a situation by necessity includes the individuals stuck in it, and individuals by necessity exist in situations.

There is no basis for the distinction except in reverse: to fabricate and use distinctions as a means to justify pre-existing normative principles. This will lead me to the second dogma at issue but first I want to deal with some possible objections to the above analysis.

A.   Milgram Study

Maybe I am being too logical. Perhaps, I should use in my analysis realistic events, after all, it is called critical realism. So, perhaps I should contemplate the examples used in the Situation that instead of defining or giving criteria for defining the distinction supposedly realistically show by example the fundamental cleavage between dispositional and situational in action. The only problem in using the examples the Situation or critical realism gives to try to understand the distinction in action is that the examples are so painful to read from the perspective of an experienced trial attorney or by anyone with any sense of honest analytical ability. The examples used are a hodgepodge of arbitrary and random hearsay taken from arbitrary and random fields of study varying from anthropology to zoology selected and selectively described in piecemeal fashion without regard to their soundness or validity solely to prove the distinction. It is sad not only that it is the latest fad for law professors to do this but that doing so is now somehow considered high academic art. Regardless, I will analyze two of the examples from the Situation that will serve to illustrate the pattern of their unsound, invalid reasoning. Any reader of this essay, if any, can use this pattern then to analyze any of the remainder dozens of unsound and invalid examples.

I will start with the often cited example of the Milgram Study. The Milgrim Study was done in the early 60's by a Yale University Professor Stanley Milgram. I will assume that this was a fundamentally sound, valid scientific study — this is an unlawyerly assumption that critical realists always make when using this Study though this troubles me but does not seem to bother them. Gina Perry, a psychologist and journalist from Australia, after studying the original papers, testing, audio, and results archived at Yale University concluded and has written in "Behind the Shock Machine: The Untold Story of the Notorious Milgram Psychology Experiments" that the Study was so fundamentally unsound and invalid that portions should be considered a hoax and that Milgram knew it. According to this psychologist (and many others out there), the

173

Milgram Study is worthless in terms of making conclusions about human nature. Professors Hanson and Yosifon, who to my knowledge are not psychologists nor psychiatrists, assume it was scientifically sound and valid so I will assume it is also.

First, as a trial lawyer, I want to deal with the humanity of the Study. As the Situation admitted, Milgram knowingly and intentionally conducted tests on human subjects by false pretenses without their informed consent, in fact lying to them in order to get consent for the acts he took, while knowing that it will cause them emotional harm and most likely resulting physical harm without any need for it. Despite this admission, critical realists have no problem with using this Study to support their argument. Supposedly, the purpose of the study was to discover why concentration camp operators would follow orders to kill the inmates. If this was the purpose, the answers were readily available in the same way historians answer this question: by looking at the historical records and interviewing the survivors. The answer is also readily available simply by the fact that the Study occurred and is still being used in academia more than forty years later: because there are people in the world who are willing to use human subjects for experiments regardless of harm and deceit practiced on the subjects and there are others out there willing to use the results of the experiments for their needs. This answer also does not seem to bother any critical realist including the authors of the Situation. According to Ms. Perry, even 40 years later some of the subjects state they have not recovered from the Study. Thus, right off the bat, from a lawyerly perspective, there is a serious credibility problem in contemplating Milgram as a basis for understanding the "situational influences" and "individual dispositions" distinction. Also, from a lawyerly perspective, using it as substantive argument seems to create a serious credibility for critical realism's claim that they are a more humane school of thought than law and economics, but whatever. I am just a lowly ham and eggar trial attorney. No doubt the esteemed academics of my *alma mater* Harvard Law School understand ethics and morality much more than my feeble mind.

In the Situation, the analysis of the Milgram Study begins by pointing out that students and professionals who were told about the experiment before it was conducted or before they learned the results predicted that only about one in a hundred teachers would go to the full range of electric shock application ordered by the experimenters. It turned out, 65% went the full range. So, aha, the professors exclaim at page 162 of the Situation, "[t]he naive predictions themselves reveal the gross extent to which we underestimate the power of the situation and wrongly presume that behavior is motivated by disposition." This makes no sense. Based on their apparently sheltered life

174

experience (situation?), the students and professionals reached a naive view that based on the facts told them the probable result is one in 100. (The struggling kids with whom I grew up, the men with whom I served in the military, and most of my clients would have given Milgram a radically different cynical prediction to the other extreme.) The new experience of the Study, now added to their life situation, has proven their prediction wrong. So, how are the prior experiences dispositional and the latter situational? Based on my poker playing experience and knowledge, I expect an ace to be dealt one in 13 cards in draw poker. During the course of a night's play, I notice it is happening much more often to an opposing player. Whatever conclusion I reach about this inconsistency, it does not make the conclusion situational and my predictions dispositional — my conclusions and predictions both before and after are all based on life and the nature of probability.

Their argument of the Situation seems to be that people should be nice. This is a normative argument combined with emotional disappointment at the failure of people to comply with the norm. It is a dogmatic belief that our norms are based on facts; I will discuss this dogma next in this essay. It is not any basis for a jurisprudence or even empirical distinction between situational and dispositional attributes. Whether we define individuals as "nice" depends on their acts in any given situation. There is no way to differentiate "nice" individuals from situations in which we deem them having acted in a way we define as "nice"; in fact, it is only through their acting "nice" in situations that we define them as nice.

Later on at page 168, the Situation seems to get back to the point yet misses the point. After pointing out that the students and professionals underestimated the percentage of persons who would go to the full electric shock, an experiment was done in which the students and professionals were told the results and then told it will be repeated but without an experimenter telling the teachers how high to go on the electric shocks. This time around, as life experience would have easily predicted, having their naivete about human nature already destroyed, the students and professionals overestimated the number of teachers who would go to the full range of electric shock. Again, aha, exclaim the professors, the "students persisted in believing that the teachers in Milgram's original experiment were motivated by a stable disposition rather than the situation of the experiment." Where does that conclusion come from? Initially, based on their life situation, they underestimated. Now, with these new facts added to their situation, they overestimated. This is not any basis for a jurisprudence or empirical distinction between situational and dispositional attributes. The over or under estimation is not made on any disposition that is independent of life experience or situation; the professors are not arguing the existence of *a priori* synthetic truths. So, what is their argument?

Again, in a very unscientific and thoughtless manner, as they do with all of their examples, the professors are injecting their normative beliefs into their conclusions and hiding them through a non-existent distinction of attributes. The "dispositional attribute" to which the professors reference is a preference, influence, or disposition either for following or for not following orders from authority. The "situational attribute" is the presence of authority giving orders. So, what does it mean to have a preference either for following or for not following orders from authority? It means when an authority gives you orders, you either follow the orders in the situation of getting them or you do not follow the orders in the latter situation. There is no "preference" existing in the individual just as there is no "intent" existing in the individual distinct from what they are saying or acting. What is really going on is that the authors of the Situation in hindsight with full knowledge of all results concluded that once the experimenter was removed as an authority leaving only the audio and paper instructions as the authority, the experimenters would be less likely to comply with authority and the students and professionals "should" have known that. This is a nice comment in hindsight having seen both sets of results. Whether the professors in reality, if they were actually involved at the time of having the naive expectations of humanity destroyed, would have been so accurate in their predictions without knowing the results as they expect the students and other professionals should have known is another matter that they ignore because it does not help their normative argument. Is this arrogance by them in stating what the students should have known dispositional or situational caused by their status as arrogant professors of law?

The most obvious example of the professors' sleight-of-hand introduction of their personal normative principles into falsely entitled scientific experiments in order to create the illusory situational/dispositional distinction is their "Good Samaritan" experiment at page 173 of the Situation conducted upon Princeton Theological Seminary students. Again, without examining the premises, method, and verification of the experiment, I will make the unlawyerly assumption that the experiment and conclusions were fundamentally sound and accurate as did the professors. The parable of the Good Samaritan in its basic form teaches and predicts that under the right circumstances, 2/3 of the people are hypocrites: what they say and what they do are in contradiction. (It is sad to realize this Parable is more of a scientific statement than most anything you will find in either law and economics or critical realism gospels.) Prior to the experiment, the students answered a survey as to why they were religious. As divinity students, as could be expected, they all gave religious reasons for doing it such as wanting to help others, personal salvation, or the salvation of humanity. At this point, the professors add yet other attribute without criteria or definition, "dispositional helping norms". How are "dispositional helping norms" in anyway different from "dispositional influences" or from "situational" helping norms? They do not say so I will assume they are not.

They further infer from the stated "dispositional helping norms" that the students should know the truth: when faced with a conflict between talking with a homeless man to see if he wants help and doing an appointed lecture to waiting students in a timely manner, the correct choice in this conflict is to forget about the students and to instead talk to the homeless man. This required resolution of the conflict, is it the professors' "dispositional" helping norm or is it a "situational" helping norm? They do not say. How did the authors decide that the correct choice of conflicting options was to "help" the homeless man by talking to him instead of giving "help" to the students by talking to them? It appears this decision was made solely because supposedly that is what the authors would do or expect be done though there is no hint that they were ever deceitfully tested on what they would do as the non-consenting students were tested. (Again, the morality of this deceit for supposed scientific purposes does not seem to bother any of the academics involved.)

As the Good Samaritan Parable accurately predicted, assuming the same definition of "help" and the same correct choice of conflicting options as assumed by the academics, the students involved in the experiment were hypocrites. As an overall average, when faced with the conflicting choice of doing their assigned job of helping students or of helping a homeless man, about 2/3 did their assigned job. At this point, we see not only what bad lawyers the authors of the Situation are but also what bad logicians they are. They again conclude as a supposedly obvious answer, aha, see the "situational" factor of "time" negated their "dispositional" factor of religious belief. Hello, have you not read the only scientific statement before you? The prediction was and the results verify that 2/3 of these students are hypocrites. Those written "dispositional helping norms" are not really their "dispositional helping norms". What they wrote is either a lie, a mistake, or a delusion. In reality, again this is supposed to be critical realism, the "dispositional helping norm" of 2/3 of them is that when faced with such a conflicting situation in life, they would rather help students than lose time with a homeless man — the results also just told you that. So, if there is a distinction between "dispositional helping norms" and "situational" influences, they do not appear here in fact.

Is there any empirical distinction in the Princeton test between this new version of dispositional influences called "dispositional helping norms" and "situational influences" such as "time"? Assuming the former reference statements such as "I want to help people"; "I want the meaning that religion gives to my life"; "I want personal salvation in a world of evil", so forth, how are any of these any less situational than "time". If one has any humanity in one's contemplation of life, the answer is "no." How is it humanely and rationally possible to consider "time', the fire in which humanity burns "situational", but religion, humanity's attempt to give meaning to that fire and burning, "individual". If anything, religion and religious beliefs are the situational driving force of most of human history. The fact that the professors' blinding religious faith in the secular religion that calls itself law screens their thought from this historical situation proves how inhumane and out of touch with reality law school academics have become. Empirically, is reading the Beatitudes regularly and trying to guide one's life by them any less situational than reading the clock and trying to guide one's life by what time it is? Are hermits and Buddhists who consider time an illusion and refuse to let it control their situation "situationists" or "individualists"?

Again, there is a difference in degree but there is no difference of kind for jurisprudence nor for anything. One can play with the words as much as one wants and be as cynical about religious beliefs as one wants, but the undisputed reality is that religious belief is in fact a way of living, it is a life situation, just as real as situational beliefs about "freedom of speech", "infringing on the freedom of the press", "interfering with the right to peaceably assemble", or "prohibiting the petitioning for a governmental redress of grievance" or any other "situation" beloved by academics. Calling religious belief "individual" and temporal concerns "situational" — the exact opposite of how the authors of the Situation made the distinction in the Galileo "capture" example — is intentional fabrication by its authors who see religion with the same contempt they view the practice of law.

As an old school trial attorney, what bothers me most about the Good Samaritan test is not the logic errors but the inhumanity of it that goes completely unnoticed by academics. It is doubtful that the authors of the Situation would not object to anyone deceitfully testing them for levels of hypocrisy; however, they have no problem with human testing upon divinity students in the name of science.

Just as in the "gun to the head" case, applying dispositional/situational distinctions to the Good Samaritan test adds nothing but unnecessary, useless complexity to an already complex problem thus hindering, delaying, and defrauding any search for truth. In terms of basic logical analysis, the only difference between "dispositional" and "situational" is a person's pragmatic choice of expression for answers to questions. The distinction for purposes of jurisprudence and policy decisions in law is worthless and adds no more information than the answers or any associated acts taken as they are. If critical realists or any academics really want to be and act like "scientists" with a scientific method, they should apply Ockham's Razor to this dogmatic distinction and disregard it.

IV.   LAW AND ECONOMICS

Legal academics pursuing the school of thought called law and economics instead of being lawyers want to be economists supposedly because they want to make legal policy the same way that scientists make scientific decisions, but they want to do so without bothering to understand how scientists make scientific decisions or even if economics is a science. Just as with their opponents in critical legal studies or whatever the recent version of that fad may call itself, they love making up theories, words, and a vast amount of verbiage that serves no purpose in jurisprudence except to hide the normative intentions that are causing them to generate those theories, words, and verbiage. The individual influence/situational influence distinction exists in law and economics in many forms created and developed through the decades (the "market", choice theory, action theory, rational choice theory, so forth) trying to hide the fact that in essence they think the same way the critical realists think. All these nominal forms are all based on the same foundational premise: there are individual influences/choices and situational influences/choices but for jurisprudence to be on a sound scientific basis, we must assume the latter exist as an objective empirical sum, set, or collection of individual influences/choices. Just as in critical legal studies, because there is no way to make the individual influence/situational influence meaningful or objective, this law and economics foundation premise states nothing meaningful for jurisprudence except in reverse — based on the speakers' intentions just as with critical realism.

Take for example again the simplest of problems in jurisprudence: gun-to-the-head. Situationally, the only available options are: a rational individual would assume the gun was loaded until proven otherwise and thus would be forced to act as ordered; an irrational individual would choose not to care whether it was loaded or would call the other person's bluff thus risk life and limb ignoring the gun. Obviously, the argument goes, legal policy and jurisprudence should exclude the irrational options and be based on the rational option. Fine, so how do we use these criteria for future jurisprudence decisions? You cannot because there is no way to define any criteria for future use that will differentiate between what the "rational" choice is and what the "irrational" choice would be from this example or any example or even theoretically. In this simple example, the "rational" choice is to assume the gun is loaded. However, "rational" choice is defined as follows: being rational means that when someone points a gun at you, you will assume it is loaded until proven otherwise. Irrational is defined as assuming the gun is not loaded. In either case, the situation is not really a collection of three individual choices but the individual choices are defined by situations that are in turn defined by individual choices and so forth. We can go on for days with this circular reasoning just as contemplated above with critical legalism. The definition and criteria for the distinction are decided by a normative decision that was already made not by any fundamental distinction in the sense experience.

Using game theory, decision theory, or any mathematical model does not help law and economics on this issue. Look at the most basic of game theory problems, the Prisoners' Dilemma:

> Two members of a criminal gang are arrested and imprisoned. Each prisoner is in solitary confinement with no means of communicating with the other. The prosecutors lack sufficient evidence to convict the pair on the principal charge. They hope to get both sentenced to a year in prison on a lesser charge. Simultaneously, the prosecutors offer each prisoner a bargain. Each prisoner is given the opportunity either to: betray the other by testifying that the other committed the crime, or to cooperate with the other by remaining silent. The offer is:
>
> If A and B each betray the other, each of them serves two years in prison
> If A betrays B but B remains silent, A will be set free and B will serve three years in prison
>   (and vice versa)
> If A and B both remain silent, both of them will only serve one year in prison (on the lesser charge)

Theoretically, according to the distinction at issue, this is a situation in which two individuals have three individual choices to make. This is nonsense to anyone with any humanity. There may be two individuals involved but their life is in the hands of forces behind their control and most likely they have spent their whole life in situations beyond their control — as the vast majority of both criminals and law-abiding citizens do. For example, the hidden forces are: their level of education; living in a society in which their acts are criminal instead of legal or just civil violations; those with power over them want to imprison them; prosecutors have options on plea agreements or prosecution; police have options on arrest or not to arrest; and so forth. Theoretically, one can make and use a probability matrix from the available choices to make some predictions as to what choices the individuals may make, but to say that the matrix is a "situational" influence in jurisprudence for use in policy decisions made up of "individual" choices for making "individual" choices is a meaningless distinction. This matrix as with any probability matrix is worthless for predicting what will happen and, most important, what ought to happen given the reality of life.

One can make multiple matrixes for each of the individual choices that got the prisoners to the point of being imprisoned and call each one a matrix if one wanted to do so. Which real experiences or possible experiences in life are a "situational" matrix to be considered for jurisprudence or policy decisions and which are to be ignored as "individual" preferences or choices are decided based upon the intentions of the creator of the matrix. Trying to use more complex mathematical models in more complex situations only makes it easier to hide there is no situational/individual distinction. Unlike the inanimate numbers that make up statistical reality, the conscious entities that make up legal reality are aware of their existence and can fight to change it.

Again, if law and economics or any academics really want to be and act like "scientists" acting with a scientific method, they should apply Ockham's Razor to this dogmatic distinction and disregard it.

V. NORMATIVE STATEMENTS CANNOT BE INFERRED FROM STATEMENTS ABOUT EXPERIENCE.

Despite centuries old Hume's Law and a century of modern physics, both critical realism/critical legal studies and law and economics without explanation and without any attempt at analytical justification assume they can infer from statements about experience, from what "is", to normative statements, to what "ought" to be. It is dogma that they can infer such because, as the Honorable Steven Shavell at my *alma mater* told me in response to my inquiry on this issue, otherwise we will have nihilism. Such ignorant, closed mindedness, with no intellectual creativity is what I have learned to expect from law school academics. Jurisprudence has gotten away with such dogma for millennia. Now that the world population is 80% literate and literacy is increasing instead of 80% illiterate as it was just a century ago, it is time for jurisprudence to eradicate such dogma and start dealing with reality as its beloved science does, or it will have more problems to deal with than just nihilism.

Lawyers wanting to be scientists are laudable in many ways given the great intellectual creation that science is but this want is also substantively delusional, cowardly, unscientific, and a failure to give the devil his due. As the Milgram and Princeton Divinity School tests in particular and life and history in general show, it does not matter to science what "ought" to be nor is it necessary for the scientific method to work that scientists know what "ought" to be or even to have an opinion on it, their concern is only with what "is". That is why supposedly lawyers and the law have the power to punish and imprison scientists and everyone else, because intellectually we supposedly do care what "ought" to be. So, jurisprudence can imitate and use science as much as it wants, but unfortunately if it is or is to be anything more than a rubberstamp of whatever "is" — be it chattel slavery or wage slavery; mercantilism or capitalism; or whatever the present threats to the soul of humanity may be — then it must accept that it will never be and can never be science.

One can play as many wordgames as one wants, but no matter how you change your syntax or semantics, there is no way to deduce nor induce from descriptive statements of "is" to conclusions expressing a new relation of an evaluative or perspective "ought". One can go from "is" statements to "is" statements, and from "ought" statements to "ought" statements. One can even play with the semantics and treat an "ought" statement as shorthand for an action that "is". For example, one can say that when dropping a rock from my hand from a tall building on earth, its acceleration due to gravity "is" 9.8 m/s/s, thus after eight seconds its velocity "ought" to be 78.4 m/s. However, in this last situation, the "is" and the "ought" are being used in the same non-evaluative descriptive "is" sense. The physicist saying what velocity ought to be is not making an evaluative judgement of the velocity but simply stating a description of what would be the empirical "is" measurement of that velocity. The physicist is not saying that the velocity ought to be 78.4 m/s because this number is morally better, ethically better, good, more utilitarian, necessary, or simply better than 84.7 m/s that is worse, bad, evil, unethical, less utilitarian, unnecessary, or immoral.

Back to the simple example of a gun pointed at one's head. You can describe the situation as detailed as you can and throw in ever possible or conceivable fact into consideration but there is no way to go from what there is to what jurisprudence, legal policy, or the law "ought" to do about it. The ought decision is based solely on other "ought" premises. One "ought" to value life; one "ought" to value other life; one "ought" to think of their family; one "ought" not play games of bluff or gamble with their life; society "ought" not to allow such behavior; and so forth. No evaluative, judgmental, or perspective conclusion whatsoever may be validly inferred from any set of purely factual premises. Trying to do so in more complicated problems by using more convoluted reasoning, semantics, or syntax — in any language whether purely linguistic or mathematical — does not change this reality. No matter how economically, rationally, mathematically efficient certain facts may be pragmatically or however, there is no basis to empirically or rationally conclude from those facts or any facts that they "ought" to be. There will always be this fundamental, substantive, essential cleavage between science and law.

All science is a conceptual tool for predicting future experience using past experience. Law is a conceptual tool for creating normative principles not from empirical facts, this is impossible, but solely from other normative principles that themselves have no logical relation to any empirical facts. The reality of human language and thought is that normative principles that foster a free, open, and prosperous society cannot be derived from the empirical experience that is a free, open, and prosperous society. The language fabric of jurisprudence impinges on experience only at the edge of the dagger hidden beneath the fabric: enforcement. For lawyers and jurisprudence to ignore this reality and the sense of responsibility and humility that should come with it by hiding as scientists is dishonest and cowardly.

VI. THE FUTURE OF LAW, NIHILISM, SCIENCE, AND THE ART OF LAWYERING

I have no problem with admitting that as an attorney I am a dinosaur, perhaps rightly so and for the good of humanity's future. In the present, for the small 1 percent of attorneys that are rainmakers or judges, being a lawyer is being a politician lacking the courage to run for office. This one percent defend their fiefdoms of power from which they look down on *hoi polloi* in the same way that all demigods in all ages guarded their power: with concern for nothing other than protecting that power. There is a small 5% or less who, as I did, practice in court. For these few, civil trials and now even arbitrations and mediations are a luxury for the rich unless one's client falls into a small class of "dead baby" or "quad" cases or their equivalent. Criminal trials are the last desperate acts of the rich, truly guilty, or truly innocent. Heaven have mercy on the latter and on truly injured plaintiffs because the legal system will not and does not really care about either despite its marketing that it does care, marketing serving only to give clients unrealistic expectations of what their attorney can do for them. In both cases, the law is what the judge decides it is on any given day and the rules of evidence are actually one rule: what does the judge want to hear as evidence on any given day. If an attorney practices in this existentialist play that is the court system as a solo trial practitioner with a sense of honesty and justice, such attorneys live a purgatory on earth that avoids being a hell only by the hope of making enough money to do something else eventually but more often freedom comes in the form of disbarment or suspension by the "overseers" running it as their plantation of serfs. To paraphrase the philosopher Arthur Schopenhauer's words regarding Hegel, on behalf of those few still practicing trial work for *hoi polloi* with a sense of humanity, humility, and honesty instead of egotism, I tell you:

> Should you ever intend to dull the wits of an intelligent person and to capacitate their brains for any king of thought whatsoever, then you cannot do better than to give them the law to study with its monstrous dishonest accumulations of words that annul and contradict one another eventually forcing their intelligence out of sheer exhaustion to accept dishonest and fraudulent thought as the normative basis for law, ethics, and morality.

Of course, the above is irrelevant because 95% of lawyers want to be either in the 1% that are rain-makers or judges or want to practice law not as lawyers but as economists, psychologists, psychiatrists, sociologists, or as anything but lawyers. These 95% practice law in the same way that the authors of the <u>Situation</u> and the lawyer-President Obama practice law which is the same way his predecessor nonlawyer-President Bush practiced law. They meet and greet, read memos, sometimes they write memos (but only as novices), and then once or twice a week or so they have a meeting to discuss what they saw and read. At these private meetings behind closed doors, they engage in confidential discussions that must be civil — no need for uncivil or irrational passions — lacking any rules of evidence, adversarial examination or cross examination, written rules of procedure or substance that are expected to be analytically followed, nor independent review by anyone other than themselves. At the end of which, they make their decision as to who will die that week, and then someone else will do the execution for them — these days the someone else is usually a computer or a machine such as a drone.

Being a lawyer makes no more difference to President Obama's decision-making process than not being one made to President Bush — it is irrelevant. They both might as well have held electricians' degrees from a trade school. It might have been better if they did, at least in that case they would have understood how drones work and thus would have known there is no such thing as "precision" bombing. Of course, the hope is that these cold-blooded decisions eventually will be made in a world lacking racism, sexism, or any "ism" not approved by the cold-blooded lawyers making the decisions. This is the Brave New World of law's future — lawyers who think and act like cold-blooded killers who happen to be lawyers or who hire lawyers to make their cold-blooded killing legal.

I have no problem with this future — though I am glad I will not be around to see it. "Killing without heroics, nothing is glorified ... nothing is reaffirmed? No heroes, no cowards, ... Only those who are left alive ... and those who are left dead." — George Patton. I grew up with cold-blooded murderers, served with some in the military, and have represented some. Realistically, they are much easier to deal with then the Machiavellian sycophants that call themselves bar overseers or the pretenders that call themselves impartial judges — at least with cold-blooded killers there exists clarity as to what to expect and how to act and respond and life goes on as long as you keep your eye on them.

It is for those presently in law school who need to decide whether this cold-blooded future as lawyers is what they want or not want and then decide what if anything to do about it — or if there is anything they can do about it. My goal here is to give a guide as to the dogma that should be rejected if you want to do anything to try to change this future and the reality of jurisprudence.

Much of this fear of accepting reality without dogma and with an admission that law's normative principles have no relation to experience has to do with jurisprudence's contempt of *hoi polloi*. When they talk about what is good for society, what the great minds of law and economics and critical legalism really mean is what is good for their social class and its view of what everyone else should be doing. From their perspective, as long as they give the commoners bread and circus, they can proceed on the work of creating the world in their image. This has worked for millennia but will soon come to an end. With 80% world literacy and 50% of the world having access to the internet with both figures rising each year, no *hoi polloi* are fooled any more by posturing that law is derived from facts. The only ones so fooled are those doing the posturing. When five conservative judges make individuals and legal fictions such as corporations equal before the law and thus negate two thousand years of Western Civilization's struggles to give meaning to individual life as distinct and as more important than simply data in an algorithm, *hoi polloi* know the judges did so as an arbitrary act to enforce their personal ethics and morality and not because any written constitution or other empirical fact requires it. At the other end, when five liberal judges redefine marriage as it has been defined throughout human history in order to allow homosexual marriage, *hoi polloi* know these judges also do so as an arbitrary act to enforce their personal ethics and morality. The thousands of pages of verbiage issued by lawyers pretending that these arbitrary decisions issue because a written constitution or other empirical fact requires their issuance does not fool *hoi polloi* but only lawyers.

For now, it does not seem to matter since the plebes are not doing anything about it. This is not good and should be of serious concern to any lawyer who still has some sense of humanity and sense of history. All of the people know they are being fooled all of the time but do not care enough to do anything about it as long as society remains economically prosperous, or at least more prosperous than the rest of the world. This is not respect for law but a fear of it. "There is respect for law, and then there is complicity in lawlessness." — Rebecca MacKinnon. For example, according to statistics, 48% of Americans believe abortion is morally equivalent to baby killing yet they do nothing about it out of respect for the majesty of the law that they morally believe is killing babies. Considering that abortion has been legal for more than 40 years at the rate of 1,000,000 abortions a year, the total is now 40,000,000 baby kills. If 48% of Americans do nothing about babies they know are being killed because the killing is legal, should I expect them to stop concentration camp killing of adults if that ever becomes legal again? I would not. So, should I rely on the 48% who believe abortion to be a choice to stop tyranny in the future? That is, I should expect the "pro-choice" Americans who expect all other Americans to follow the law under threat of imprisonment despite any personal moral beliefs they have that the law is killing babies to be the heros against any future tyranny? I would not expect them to do anything either. So, any future battle against tyranny will depend on the 4% of the population who does not seem to care whether or not abortion is killing babies? I doubt that also.

If society is willing to let a handful of judges act as tyrants forcing their personal sense of ethics and morality upon all of society simply because they wear judicial robes, there is no reason to expect them from stopping tyrants wearing military or lab uniforms from doing the same. Supposedly, according to John F. Kennedy, "those who make peaceful revolution impossible will make violent revolution inevitable." Contempt for *hoi polloi* has always backfired in the past and being scientific about this, using the past to predict the future, I should expect something to snap in the future. I doubt it because of the present power of technology and science that was absent in the past combined with the fact that law wants to be subservient to science and technology instead of at least equal to their honesty about their reality and its consequences and how to deal with it.

Furthermore, at this point in history, as has occurred many times before, Western Civilization is again facing conflict with Eastern Civilization. Academics in both schools of jurisprudence and academics in general, except perhaps for historians, take for granted the struggles that have led up to their present freedoms. They assume as undisputedly true the value of such intellectual concepts as formal logical systems, republican and democratic systems of governance, equality before the law, and analytical thought but also assume as inevitable underlying unstated spiritual ones that supposedly have been assumed into secular law such as the Beatitudes and a Christian concept of love and mercy as being more important than justice. Historically, these foundational aspects of Western Civilization taken for granted by law school academics and most academics, except perhaps by historians, seem to have occurred accidentally and would have disappeared from history at numerous times when they came into conflict with Eastern

Civilization emphasizing mysticism, authority, order, and hierarchy but for *hoi polloi* fighting on behalf of Western ideals.

Law school academics assume, again law school academics are always making unlawyerly assumptions, that in any assimilation between Western and Eastern Civilization that Western normative principles respecting intellectual concepts of formal logical systems, republican and democratic systems of governance, equality before the law, analytical thought, the Beatitudes, and a Christian concept of love and mercy that supposedly have been assumed into their secular religion will prevail. Based on my reading of history, I do not see how this assumption can be made other than by expecting pure dumb luck will always be on our side.

The days of *hoi polloi* willing to fight to defend Western Civilization are gone and rightly so. If there is a future battle for the soul of Western Civilization, it will be fought by machines and the professionals hired to run them. This will mean it lost its soul anyway so who cares who wins. More likely, it is going to have to stand and prove itself as a better alternative or as part of an assimilation with Eastern Civilization. I do not see Millennials or their offspring, if any, going into battle to defend Western Civilization. Maybe I am wrong but I doubt it. Western law will either have to be honest about what it is doing and how so that *hoi polloi* see humanity, hope, and meaning in it for them; or, it will have to start relying on machines and what essentially will be mercenaries or cold-blooded killers to protect it — as appears to be starting to occur now with the use of drones and private security companies to do the law's killing for it.

If Western law continues to work as a secular religion enforcing the ruling class ideology of a handful of judges and a *1984*-like Inner Party behind a screen of delusional law and fake economics and critical legalism distinctions and normative principles pretending to be facts, this puts it on the same rational foundation and teleological process as any North Korean or any totalitarian legal system, and thus if history is a guide it will eventually become one. Democracies and republics have come and gone in history with a predictable pattern even in the absence of the power of science and technology. So much so that the philosopher Plato became history's first known sociologist by studying their rise and fall and creating a life cycle for such: they start with a kingship; then a timocracy or plutocracy in which jealous noblemen struggle for the King's wealth and power; then oligarchy; then democracy; finally, democracy collapses into a tyrant. Assuming it can, how does jurisprudence try to stop this life cycle into tyranny in the present reality of science and technology instead of aiding it by accepting tyrants hiding behind a screen of dogma and an associated contempt for the actual practice of law?

I do not want to be a hypocritic by exclaiming errors to everyone and then failing to give any real alternatives as the authors of the <u>Situation</u> did. There are thousands of options for making jurisprudence theoretically and pragmatically up-to-date into the modern world of science and technology if academics in law would look for such options instead of wasting time on worthless dogma. Unfortunately, jurisprudence is so many centuries behind the reality of our modern world and in need of so much update, it is almost impossible to say where to start. To paraphrase Kant, it is time it "awoke from a long dogmatic slumber" and does anything to deal with its reality; it is better than doing nothing as essentially it is doing now. Some improvements are forced upon jurisprudence by technology and science. The only significant change that has increased modern legal culture's fact finding accuracy when compared to older traditions is its use of technology such as DNA testing. Otherwise it would be still stumping around in the dark no better than medieval trials by ordeal or jury trials in Rome's *Basilica Julia*. It is dangerous to expect technology to force changes in jurisprudence, it is supposed to be the other way around when it comes to deciding how society "ought" to be.

Theoretically, conceptually, and pragmatically, I want to propose simple updates for now. They are as follows.

A.   No Fear of Nihilism

Responding to this essay contemplation by calling me a nihilist is intellectually and realistically unsound and cowardly. Doing so while pretending to be a scientist is also hypocritical and delusional. Science has been dealing with similar problems in its language and concepts for at least a century and philosophers for two millennia before this. According to some scientists and philosophers, nihilism may be the next evolution of humanity. Most of these forecasters do not fear it but welcome it. As philosophers have known from antiquity, nihilism does not negate truth but only meaning. The moment a nihilist states "there is no truth", they have just contradicted themselves and proven there is truth. The negation of meaning plus the power of technology and science may be the ultimate good finally giving humanity freedom to choose meaning for their lives if we can control it. Jurisprudence is a search for truth not meaning in life. It should

190

not be threatened by nihilism. If we cannot control them, technology and science will be humanity's new slave master making all of us just data in the algorithms used by any future *1984*-like Inner Party to run the world. So, if your instinctive response is nihilism and ignorance, you need to get over it.

B. Science

In trying to make law into a "social science", academics are in fact cheapening it. If law school academics who are wannabe social scientists would actually study and contemplate the nature of the social sciences, they would conclude as most who have studied and made this contemplation have concluded, that the social sciences are sciences in the same way that the Dewey Decimal System and West's Topic and Key Number System may be considered science. They organize complicated and convoluted facts into an organized system allowing for subsequently locating the facts based on one's needs for them. Such organization and categorization are important, difficult, and challenging tasks but they are not the same conceptual or pragmatic tasks faced by law that must create and enforce normative rules upon facts to maintain a free, open, and prosperous society without being able to deduce or induce those rules from the facts.

Science itself is radically different and faces bigger hurdles then simply organization in its attempts to predict future events just as law does in trying to make and enforce normative principles that foster a free, open, and prosperous society without being able to derive those normative principles from the empirical experience that is a free, open, and prosperous society. Thus, I have no problem in admiring science, respecting it, and in trying to understand it and we should do all of these. We have to do so as lawyers; science is the present and the future. However, if we are to learn anything from the scientific method, we should do so as it exists now not as it existed in the world of Galileo. Scientists live in a world of uncertainty not certainty as amateur scientists in law school academia seen to assume in their desire to be scientists instead of lawyers.

Approximately a hundred years ago, through the development of quantum mechanics scientists were forced to accept the empirical fact that the reality they study is made not of fixed physical objects existing in time and space but of abstract mathematical concepts. In the case of quantum mechanics, the mathematical concepts consist of waves called probability waves. Almost overnight, physics changed from a study of absolute certainty to one of merely predicting the odds on behavior that is random on a whole different level not possible in classical physics and that never can be predicted. This wave "collapses" or is "ruptured" when it is observed at which point the probability of its being detected in any other place suddenly becomes zero and it becomes a particle. Until observation, the particle's position is inherently uncertain and unpredictable and unknown. Because there is no way to define the exact point at which such a collapse occurred, scientists have had to discard the laws governing individual events in favor of the present pragmatic conceptualization of physics in which there is no deep quantum reality, no actual world of electrons and photons, only a description of the world in a formalism that it can use to predict and manipulate events and the properties of matter. Thus to a scientist, asking the question of where a photon or any subatomic particle was before it was observed is not a question that can be asked but a meaningless question similar to asking "is this false statement true"?

Science did not end with this fundamental cleavage in the nature of reality. Science accepted it as reality, created concepts such as "wave-particle duality", and has gone on to bigger problems. Until its reality changes, this fundamental cleavage in science will remain and is not and will not be the end of science.

Therefore, if jurisprudence does really want to be scientific, the fundamental cleavage between normative "ought" statements that are the substance of law and empirical "is" statements that impinge on it only at the point of enforcement of the "ought" statements are not the end of jurisprudence, it is the beginning. This reality has not been forced upon jurisprudence almost overnight as it was upon science. Jurisprudence has had centuries to accept and deal with it but is still in denial. The beginning is to acknowledge it. Thereafter, we can begin to discuss the possibilities as to what to do with this fundamental truth.

The most significant possibility is to finally admit that law is the same as ethics: it is ethics with a monopoly on the power to enforce its ethical conclusions. This is reality. Denying this truth while science and technology continue to accept and deal with its realities and uncertainties is only further weakening law's ability to have any control over either. It is only fear of nihilism and *hoi polloi* revolting violently in the streets that is barring this admission.

If I ever have to attend a pre-trial conference again, it would be the happiest moment of my professional career if the judge came out and said:

I have decided to stop pretending that my decisions will be decided by anything other than my personal ethics and morality. To guide the ethical and moral decisions that I will make in this case, I will use the normative principles of John Rawls' "A Theory of Justice" to guide my decisions and therefore you may question my decisions and argue and submit evidence with those principles in mind.

Or, in the alternative, it would make be equally happy if the judge said:

I have decided to stop pretending that my decisions will be decided by anything else than my personal ethics and morality. To guide the ethical and moral decisions that I will make in this case, I will use the normative principles of Robert Nozick's "Anarchy, State, and Utopia" to guide my decisions and therefore argue and submit evidence with those principles in mind.

Anything would be better than continuing the farce of pretending that there is a thing called "law" distinct from the ethics and morality of the person deciding what "law" is and how it will be executed.

C. The Art of Lawyering

As the use of DNA testing in law has shown, much improvement in the law can occur through application of technology and thus a significant part of lawyering can be made a science. Eliminating the adversary process in an area of law such as divorce to instead use algorithms to plug numbers into a computer and have it generate decisions would be a vast improvement over the present mess of a "monstrous dishonest accumulations of words that annul and contradict one another". However, there is no way around the reality that eventually in some areas of law the cleavage between normative decisions and empirical reality will require law and lawyering to be an art — that is unless tyranny takes over completely, kills all lawyers as unnecessary, and law become tyranny's dogma. The art of handling the fundamental disconnect between normative principles and empirical reality requires both analytical abilities and an emotional personal sense of empathy and humanity; procedures to control and guide them; and the experience to control and guide them. This is a difficult combination of talents. It requires education and learning but most importantly it requires life experience in a diversity of mental and physical challenges to the required analytical and emotional abilities and in the application of the education and learning.

A first step for making the art of lawyering work in the present and ready for the future, even if it never was but wants to be, is to accept as science has accepted Ockham's Razor as an epistemological, metaphysical, and heuristic preference. A scientist given a choice between using the following calculations or formula in theories would always use the first option:

$1 + 1 = 2$

$((1 + 4) \times (2 + 2)) + 6 - (2 \times 5) - (2 \times 7) = 8 + 4 - 5 - 5$

Lawyers working on an hourly basis and judges, especially appellate judges, will always use the latter because they believe the first option is too simple and thus would degrade the appearance that they do difficult work while the latter formula makes them appear smarter than most attorneys and most people. So, despite the fact that the answer is the same for both, in law the powers almost always take advantage of any attempt to complicate matters as the preferred option.

A second step would be a heuristic preference to be consistent on simple inductions and deductions to establish credibility at least for the much more convoluted and subtle arguments in which inconsistencies will unavoidably occur. A philosophy professor once told me that "consistency is the sign of a shallow mind." That is probably true in complex logic contemplating the nature of the universe but philosophers can say this because they are always trying to be logically consistent and are so when faced with relatively simple problems. This is not true of law as exemplified throughout the Situation and in the foundational concepts of law and economics.

For example, the Situation claims that "regulatory capture" is a scientifically proven true axiom: regulatory agencies, even when created to act in the public interest, will eventually always advance the commercial or political concerns of special interest groups that dominate the industry or sector they are charged with regulating. Given this problematic truth, what is critical realism's solution to it? It wants to create a Department of Consumer and Regulatory Affairs to regulate commercial and political concerns. But wait. According to the truth you just gave me, will not this agency eventually always advance the commercial and political concerns of special interest groups that dominate the industry or sector it is charged with regulating despite its initial intent to act in the public interest? No, because we put "consumer" in the title of the agency so that the axiom we just discovered does not apply. If it is that simple, why not save the money that would be spent on yet another government regulatory agency by adding "consumer" to the title of all the other regulatory agencies? This is the kind of inconsistent nonsense from critical realism making jurisprudence seem as a joke to anyone thinking clearly.

Law and economics is not any better with its simplest axioms. The great and honorable Richard Posner pontificates, "I do not myself believe that many people do things think they are the right thing to do ... I do not think that knowledge of what is morally right is motivational in any serious sense for anyone except a handful of saints". So, what is his method of dealing with this problematic truth? We must appoint him and all other similarly judgmental persons for life tenure as judges with complete immunity for their decisions and with no accountability to anyone for their decisions in which: 1) they pass normative judgments on the miserable souls before them; 2) do so by pretending they are complying with "law"; 3) hide the fact that behind the scenes they are really making their decisions based on undisclosed "economic" principles; 4) while also allowing them to make money and prestige writing books based on their saintly position. What a bunch of hypocritical, inconsistent, pompous, sycophants whose primary success has been to destroy the credibility of jurisprudence for anyone but the rich they serve.

Part of the problem trying to make this art workable, if it ever was, is law school's disconnect from reality. Part of its student body wants to be economists, psychologists, psychiatrists, sociologists, or anything but lawyers. They quickly get bored or disinterested in the basics of lawyering such as evidence, procedure, substantive law, statutes, common law, and the adversarial process of examination and cross-examination. In fact, they consider the passions that unavoidably occur and result in the examination and cross-examination of normative principles to be uncivil, uncouth, and mean. The few that want to learn evidence, procedure, case law, and statutory law and the adversarial process of examination and cross-examination quickly become bored with the classroom analysis of concepts that can only be learned by practice. Most of the reasonably good attorneys that I have known from either category stopped going to class by their second year of law school. One could learn just as much by reading Emanuel Law Outlines and save paying six figures on tuition. By failing to educate each category of law students adequately, the end result is lousy lawyering and lousy economists, psychologists, psychiatrists, sociologists, and so forth.

We have to do something about this. Either make law school a one year trade school in which an entrance requirement is a Ph.D. in another field of study or split the curriculum up into two paths of study. One would essentially consist of a dual major in which at the end of three years a student gets a Ph.D. in their preferred field of economics, psychology, psychiatry, sociology, or whatever plus a degree in basic law. The other would start out with a year of intensive and critical study of Emanuel Law

Outlines and then two years of intensive mock trial and moot court competition testing and applying the students' humanity and empathy, logic and investigative abilities, and aggressiveness with analytical and investigation skills so that hopefully these skills are allowed to strengthen and flourish. With trial practice in all its forms rapidly disappearing from the real world, there is really no other way to learn the art of lawyering except in intensive, detailed, and realistic mock trial and moot court competition.

If we really want to make modern law a "profession" as that term was intended to be used originally as the equivalent of religious vows and not as a front to give credibility to business and academic tenure ambitions, we should contemplate its initial roots in modern Western Civilization, learn from those roots, update them, and apply them to the fundamental crevice between the enforced normative principles of jurisprudence and empirical reality. Law degrees were the first degrees to be granted in the earliest development of the university concept in the Middle Ages at the University of Bologna in the 13th Century. However, at that time, emphasis was law as philosophy and theology. Law was considered the study of ethics and morals operating in the context and means of secular government. Since this is what law really is, the ethics and morals of judges completely distinct from empirical reality which they enforce by a monopoly of violence, the one Ph.D. or at least Master's Degree that every law student should get prior to law school graduation is one in ethics and morality.

Also, in the practice of law, there needs to be separation from areas that need the rare combination of abilities to empathize with all aspects of the human condition while also being aggressive enough to conduct adversarial examination and cross-examination — that is a separation between those areas that need the art of lawyering and those that do not. For most arbitrations, meditations, rule-making, even litigation of most civil matters, an inquisitorial process even one handled by non-lawyer professions familiar with the subject matter at issue would be better than an adversary process by lawyers — especially these days in which billable hour billing is the primary method of earning a living for lawyers in such areas. The more time is spent on a problem, the more money for the lawyers.

This billable hour billing problem has adverse effects that escalate almost exponentially until it does more in practice to destroy the credibility of jurisprudence and especially its adversarial process than anything else. Since there is no incentive financially to apply Ockham's Razor to simplify either the facts or the theory at issue in a case but only to complicate matters, there is no incentive to hire, train, or promote

196

lawyers that can think logically and clearly to the substance and essence of a problem — such would only result in less pay for the lawyer and law firm. Lawyers that can think efficiently, logically, and clearly to the substance and essence of a problem do not succeed financially in the billable hour machine that is most firm practice especially big firm law practice nor gain credibility among their peers — consisting primarily of those who can generate paper and convolute any issue to the determent of thinking logically or clearly. They thus do not become influential lawyers, judges, and law professors such as those who wrote the <u>Situation</u>. These powers-that-be in law and jurisprudence in turn expect the same wasteful verbiage they issued as attorneys that got them their influence and appointment to the powers-that-be and thus the nonsense continues.

Except for felony criminal cases and civil cases against the government or government officials, there is really no need for the adversarial process. However, in the cases where it is needed, when representing the defendant in a felony criminal case or the plaintiff against the government, the attorneys should be the most aggressive, competent advocates available.

This is an outline of possible conceptual and practical updates to jurisprudence. They have no chance of being accepted or even of being acknowledged until jurisprudence stops being dogmatic and accepts the reality that it is simply ethics and personal morality with a monopoly on violence to enforce its normative conclusions.

VI. CONCLUSION / SLAVERY

The authors of the <u>Situation</u> end it in the same way it began: by lecturing to their readers on their need to be better persons. At this end, not satisfied with condemning the living, they now go into the past and condemn the dead as knaves and fools who allowed chattel slavery to exist as law for millennia in every human culture throughout history on every continent. Their pompous repetition of cliches about slavery repeated from popular culture and their arrogance at believing they are entitled to condemn the dead proves their true egotistical and inhumane nature. They are lousy moralists and historians in addition to being lousy lawyers — as with everything else they tried to be but lawyers. Their illogical, inhumane, and dogmatic view of jurisprudence as exemplified by their sophomoric pontification on slavery will do nothing but make jurisprudence as meaningless and as worthless in any future struggle against wage slavery and the slavery of technology as it was with chattel slavery.

The last of legal chattel slavery was outlawed in the Mideast, Asia, and African Continent in the 1970's. Until 200 years ago, chattel slavery was an accepted part of all human cultures from the simplest hunter-gathers to the most advanced civilizations as an ethical good, thus legally enforced throughout human history with rare exceptions. For lawyers to look into the past and in hindsight to condemn ethically and morally the societies and individuals who practiced chattel slavery and the law that enforced it is analogous to capitalist economics condemning the past for using barter economies or physicists looking back and condemning those who practiced Aristotelian physics or any of the physics of Copernicus, Tycho Brahe, Galileo, Descartes, or Newton. Chattel slavery was one of the means humanity for millennia used to survive and did survive in a physical world whose physical and mental struggles were beyond anything most modern individuals living in a world of technological luxury and scientific power over nature can barely comprehend let alone understand and accept nor deal with. Antiquity and many cultures even up to the mid-19th Century saw our concept of wage slavery in which a worker can be terminated and essentially thrown out into the street with his family to survive on his own without any means of support nor obligation for support from society or from anyone as much more crude, evil, and disruptive of maintaining social and cultural relationships than their concept of chattel slavery in which masters had social, ethical, legal, and moral duties to physically support the slave and the slave's family. Any modern concept that our ancestors were idiots, knaves, or fools is idiocy, knavery, and foolish. They survived and progressed human society enduring struggles that would kill most of us. The unavoidable historical reality, despairing as it may be, is that humanity survived and the authors of the Situation are here with the luxury to condemn the dead because there was slavery in the past not in spite of it. Chattel slavery was as much a normative part of social cohesion and the social fabric that kept human society fighting to survive and to progress into our present just as wage slavery is now. For anyone that wants to really contemplate slavery, its past and its future in our modern scientific and technological society, start with "Chattel Slavery v. Wage Slavery in a Technological Society" at www.betweenworldandus.com and then read real history written by real historians not by sophomoric amateurs such as the authors of the Situation guided by political correctness. We should respect the dead and have empathy for all of their suffering; do not ask for whom the bell tolls, it tolls for us and we will be joining them soon enough.

The word "slave" is derived from the "Slav", a people who migrated into Central Europe beginning in the 6th Century who suffered enslavement first by the Western and Eastern Roman Empires and then by the various Islamic empires for more than a thousand years. For a minority of enslaved individuals, tribes, and cultures such as the Carthaginians under the Roman Republic, the people of Melos by the Athenian Empire, and the Dzungar people by the Chinese Qianlong Emperor, slavery meant certain death and genocide. For a minority of other enslaved, such as Turks, Circassians, Abkhazians, Georgians, Copts, Slavs and Bulgars from Anatolia, Eastern and Central Europe, and the Balkans enslaved by Islamic Empires, it was of means of entry and eventually conquest of the enslaving culture by creating an upper ruling class of former slave Janissaries and Mamluk. For the vast majority of enslaved, such as the Gaullic and Germanic tribes enslaved by Romans for a millennium, it was a means of assimilation in which both cultures adapted, modified, and synthesized their similar and competing attributes to create new culture in a real-life Hegelian dialectical process.

For the 400,000 African slaves captured by their fellow Africans and then delivered to the American Colonies and then United States before the outlaw of the slave trade by the United States and the British Empire in 1807, slavery was without doubt not genocide nor was it a death sentence. Those 400,000 became 4,000,000 by the Civil War and the 13th Amendment and are 40,000,000 now. The future of this assimilation of cultures is dependent on us. If it is Balkanized by accepting the Ta-Nehisi Coates view that past chattel slavery is a grudge and excuse for failure handled down through the generations and centuries along with white guilt for it as the Situation prefers, a dialectic into a new and better culture will never occur. If we accept the Frederick Douglas alternative of seeing chattel slavery and wage slavery as two sides of the same coin held by all as Americans in the United States, there is hope of avoiding another century or so of wasting social resources on racism. Otherwise, we will have to fight among ourselves for another two or three generations until technology provides a solution to racism as written about in the book "Black No More" by George S. Schuyler.

Absent a cataclysm, our future and the future of jurisprudence will be in a scientific and technological society. As summarized well by the sociologist Jacques Ellul in his book "The Technological Society":

A principal characteristic of [technology] ... is its refusal to tolerate moral judgments. It is absolutely independent of them and eliminates them from its domain. Technique never observes the distinction between moral and immoral use. It tends on the contrary, to create a completely independent technical morality. ... Not even the moral conversion of the technicians could make a difference. At best, they would cease to be good technicians. This attitude supposes further that technique evolves with some end in view, and that this end is human good. Technique is totally irrelevant to this notion and pursues no end, professed or unprofessed.
...
It is not true that the perfection of police power is the result of the state's Machiavellianism or of some transitory influence. The whole structure of society of society implies it, of necessity. The more we mobilize the forces of nature, the more must we mobilize men and the more do we require order
...
...there is a limited elite that understands the secrets of their own techniques, but not necessarily of all techniques. These men are close to the seat of modern governmental power. The state is no longer founded on the 'average citizen', but on the ability and knowledge of this elite. The average man is altogether unable to penetrate technical secrets or governmental organization and consequently can exert no influence at all on the state.
...
Technique shapes an aristocratic society, which in turn implies aristocratic government. Democracy in such a society can only be a mere appearance. Even now, we see in propaganda the premises of such a state of affairs. When it comes to state propaganda, there is no longer any question of democracy.

Ellul saw hope only in Christianity to avoid the above developments from the essence of science and technology. Hopefully, jurisprudence can prove him wrong. It cannot do this if it continues to remain centuries behind science and technology both in its dogma and in its delusional denial of its nature as a fabric of language unavoidably intertwined with ethics and morality separated from fact impinging on experience only through the dagger of execution hidden beneath that fabric.

References

Page

"The Situation: An Introduction to the Situational Character,
Critical Realism, Power Economics, and Deep Capture"   4 -7, 10,
                                                                15-17,
                                                                19-21,
                                                                36, 41

Two Dogmas of Empiricism, Willard Van Orman Quine   14,

Behind the Shock Machine: The Untold Story of the
Notorious Milgram Psychology Experiments, Gina Perry   16

The Technological Society, Jacques Ellul   42, 43

The backcover page contains the logo for the *Knights of Thermopylae Inn of Court,* a non-profit whose resources were supportive and instrumental for the writing and compiling of this book: